Sing for Your Father, Su Phan

by *Stella Pevsner*
and Fay Tang

Clarion Books
New York

CHILDRENS ROOM

Clarion Books
a Houghton Mifflin Company imprint
215 Park Avenue South, New York, NY 10003
Copyright © 1997 by Stella Pevsner and Fay Tang

The type for this text is 13/16-point Berkeley.

Printed in the USA

Library of Congress Cataloging-in-Publication Data
Pevsner, Stella.
Sing for your father, Su Phan / by Stella Pevsner and Fay Tang.
     p.   cm.
Summary: Recalls the events in a North Vietnamese village that forever changed
the lives of the youngest daughter of a prosperous trader and her family.
ISBN 0-395-82267-X
[1. Family life—Vietnam (Democratic Republic)—Fiction. 2. Vietnamese
Conflict, 1961-1975—Fiction. 3. Vietnam (Democratic Republic)—Fiction.]
I. Tang, Fay. II. Title.
PZ7.P44815Shr 1997
[Fic]—dc21   97-4290
                                                  CIP
                                                  AC

BP 10 9 8 7 6 5 4 3 2 1

For my parents
John and Louise Donath
—S.P.

For my father
Phoc Menh Tang
and my mother
Nhi Mui Voong
—F.T.

When I was a very little girl in Vietnam I thought happiness was something I could always hold close. My family was loving, my father was well off, and days were spent in carefree games with my friends.

But as the years went by my simple life was shattered. This is the story of what happened to me and my family. . . .

Chapter
1

SU PHAN STOOD AT THE SHORE, gazing out to the sea. The sun, leaping across the tops of waves, flashed like slices of mirrors.

Shielding her eyes with her hand, Su Phan stared harder and harder into the distance. Perhaps by the force of her desire she could make her father's ships appear on the horizon.

"Su Phan!" her friend Lien called out. "Come over here and play."

"I can't. I must watch for him. For my father."

Lien left the others to join her friend. "Watching won't make him come back any faster."

Su Phan knew she was right. But she also knew her father was late getting back. His three ships had carried sake and incense to the port of Haiphong in the northern part of Vietnam, as always. But instead of the usual three weeks, he had now been away for four weeks.

"I must watch," Su Phan said. She wouldn't say aloud what she was thinking. *If I don't keep my gaze on the horizon he may never return.*

"Your father will come back soon," Lien said. "He always does come back, and brings you sesame candy and green bean cake."

"Yes. And he will eat his fish and rice and he will light his pipe and then he will say, 'Mui, Mui, come sing for your father.'" The word *Mui* meant *Little Girl*. "And I will stand before him and sing this Chinese song:

> "Zit gong gong ju dee tong
> Mui Mui Grai Grai
> Xeung chong fiun
> Pa Pa faun leoi Mui Mui
> Zut bout jee mah tong"

She translated the words into Vietnamese for her friend.

> *The moon is bright, bright, and lights the ground.*
> *Little girl, little girl, be good, good*
> *Go to bed and sleep*
> *Father will come back and buy little girl*
> *One bag of sesame candy*

When Su Phan had finished, Lien said, "But that is such a baby song for a girl who is almost eight."

Su Phan knew this. Her grandmother used to sing it to her when she was little. But still, her father loved to hear her sing those words while she tilted her head and did little dancing steps. "It's only because it's Chinese," she told Lien. "Remember, that's what we speak to each other at home. At least, most of the time."

Just then, the other girls called out, "Su Phan, Lien, come play the clamshell game!"

Su Phan glanced over to where her friends were drawing on the hardened earth with a stick. They would form two teams and toss clamshells toward the opposite line. They'd try to come close without going beyond the mark.

Su Phan had a supply of the pretty scalloped pink and blue shells and could probably win even more from her friends. But she hadn't the heart to play today.

"No, I must watch for my father," she answered, knowing of course that standing there wouldn't change anything. But she just couldn't leave. She pushed back her bangs; it was hot, even with the breezes from the sea.

Lien wished there were some way she could help her friend. Suddenly she said, "I have an idea! Let's pretend we have strings attached to our fingers, and they are stretching out to sea, all the way to your father's ships. We will pull those ships here to shore!"

Su Phan liked the suggestion. "Yes," she said, fanning out her fingers and holding them high in the air. "Strings, strings, pull, pull. Pull my father's ships from the sea, back here to us."

Khenh and Peng came over. "What are you doing?" they asked, staring.

Without lowering her hands, Lien said, "We have strings attached to her father's ships. We are pulling them back here to the water's edge."

"I see," Khenh said. "You're playing imaginary games, like little children."

"You can play make-believe no matter what your age," Peng pointed out. And then she stood next to Lien and raised her hands, too. Finally even Khenh joined in.

"Strings, strings, pull in the boats," they chanted.

After a while their arms got tired. "Enough of this," Khenh said. "Are we going to play the clamshell game or not?"

"All right, let's go start," Peng said.

But suddenly Su Phan gasped. "Oh, look!"

The girls stared to where she was pointing. And there, far, far in the distance, was a ship . . . no, two ships . . . no, three!

"Those are my father's ships! I know they are!" Su Phan yelled. She was certain, even though they were still just dots on the horizon. "Pull, pull!"

Laughing, all the girls stood in a row and pulled their spread-out fingers back and forth, as though hauling in a catch from the sea.

Before long, Su Phan was absolutely sure they were her father's ships. Now she could admit to herself the thing she had feared. She'd been sure the ships had gone down to the bottom of the sea, and her father and the crew with them.

Chapter 2

PROUDLY, SU PHAN WATCHED her father jump from the first ship onto the dock. He was tall and strong and his black hair lifted in the breeze.

"Father!" she cried out, rushing toward him. At the sound of her voice he turned from a crew member and held out his arms to his daughter. His teeth, when he smiled his welcome, looked very white against his tanned face. He swung her up in his arms and kissed her. His white shirt was damp, and held the smell of sweat and the sea.

Su Phan waited while her father gave orders to the crew, now unloading the cargo. Then, hand in hand, they walked to their home of bamboo and wooden planks where the family was waiting.

After many embraces the family sat in a circle around the cooking pots. They ate their dinner of rice and fish without a great deal of talking.

Then, lighting his pipe, Chung Bo called out, "Mui, Mui, come sing for your father."

Remembering what her friend Lien had said about the baby song, Su Phan stood stiffly and sang another. It was the one everyone had to sing in the morning when they entered their school, and again in the afternoon when they left.

"Em la bup mang nom,
em lon len trong mua cach mang,
suong vui co dang tien phong
co dang nhu anh thai duong."
We are young pieces of bamboo.
We grow up under Communism.
We feel good and happy.
We have Communism like sunshine—

But before she could finish, her father said angrily, "You may have to sing that song in school, but we do not praise Communism in this house. Now, go to bed."

"But Father . . ." Su Phan protested, tears coming to her eyes.

"You heard what he said!" her grandmother shouted. "Go, now!"

Su Phan looked at her mother, but Voong Nhi Mui shook her head in warning. Vietnam or China, it didn't matter. Elders must be obeyed.

Su Phan's older brother, Senh Hau, and her older sister, Su Lenh, made no move to leave.

"You, too!" the grandmother said to the sister. "Off to bed!"

Su Lenh gave her brother a look of anger but said nothing as she followed Su Phan into the area where the children and grandmother slept. When they were behind the thin curtain that separated them from the others Su Lenh said, "It's not fair. You're a little girl. But Senh Hau is only a year older than I. So I should be allowed to stay with the others."

"I am not so little," Su Phan said with a pout. "But just remember that Senh Hau is a boy and so our ah mah has always favored him."

"I don't care," her sister grumbled. "I still say it's not fair."

"Shhhh," Su Phan whispered. "Let's try to hear what they're saying." She crept from behind the curtain and along the cement floor closer to where the others still sat around the table. Since there were no windows, the only light came from a pale moon shining through the open kitchen door. The cooking fire, now embers, gave out a faint orange glow.

"Tell us now why you were so late in returning," Grandmother was saying. "We were worried that something had happened to you."

"Some of my friends said the sea dragons must have swallowed your ships," Senh Hau said to his father. "What nonsense!"

"We prayed each day for your safe return," Mother said.

Father puffed on his pipe. "We had difficulty in leaving Haiphong. The Communist authorities threatened to seize our ships and all the goods on them."

"Father!" Senh Hau said. "Were you afraid?"

"Yes, a little, at first. But then I realized that they made those threats only to get our money, not the ships."

"Did you give them your profits, Father?"

"I did. There was no other way. Still, we all felt lucky that we were allowed to continue our journey."

"You must not go again," Voong Nhi Mui said to her husband. "The Communists grow in strength each day. They have already taken away people who were friends of the French government. Now I fear they are after you."

"That is a foolish fear," her husband remarked. "Even the Communists would not touch me. They know I am not an ordinary peasant, someone to be pushed around."

"I wish I could believe what you say is true," his wife replied. There was a brief flare as she reached over and stirred the embers. "But remember, there are people here who know we have riches and are jealous. Who knows? Some could be spies who make reports to the Communist authorities."

Grandmother said, "Be quiet and listen to your husband." She flung the dregs from her tea toward the fire, and they made a hissing sound. "He knows these people and if he does not fear them, neither should we. We are only women and do not understand these things."

"Wife, don't worry," Chung Bo said. "I must continue my trade so that I can support this family. But next time I will be prepared. I will take more sake, incense, and other goods so that I can make enough to bribe the officials and still have something left. If I pay them, they will let me go on my way."

"I hope that's so," Mother murmured.

"Hush!" Grandmother said.

"The important thing," Father continued, "is that we are all in good health and together. That will not change."

Su Phan whispered to her sister, who had crept up beside her, "I am afraid."

"Afraid of what, little puppy?"

"I am afraid for our father."

"Silly girl! He is Chung Bo, the trader. He knows what he's doing. Let's go to our beds."

Reluctantly, Su Phan crept back. Once settled in her wooden platform bed, she arranged the mosquito netting around her. Gradually, the voices drifting into the room lulled her to sleep.

In the following weeks, Chung Bo made more incense than before and went to his workers and urged them to do the same. "I will need twice the amount," he said. Then he went to the sake brewers and gathered up bottles until there was no more room to store them.

The night before he was to leave again, Su Phan listened to the talk of her elders as she lay in bed. Now, even Grandmother sounded worried.

"My son," she said, her voice dropping so low Su Phan had to strain to hear the words, "are you sure you must go on this trip? There is much talk of the war now. I fear for you and for all of us."

"What do women know of war?" Chung Bo replied. "War is man's concern."

"But bombs fall on all alike," Grandmother said.

"True, but when they do fall, it is on big cities. We are just a village here."

"Haiphong, where you are going, is big."

Chung Bo sighed. "Neither the South Vietnamese nor the Americans are bombing Haiphong. What would you have me do? Give up everything for what . . . foolish village talk?"

Grandmother made no reply.

Su Phan trembled in her bed. She had heard villagers talk of the war when they didn't know she was listening. Was her family really safe in this house? And would Father return with his ships, as always?

Chapter
3

IN SPITE OF HIS BRAVE TALK, Chung Bo didn't seem his usual cheerful self as he and his men loaded the ships. Two of the sailors had refused to go again because of the danger, and new men had to be hired.

"There is no need to be afraid," Chung Bo said to the workers as they carried the goods aboard. "I have extra money to bribe people so they'll let us come and go. We'll all be back with our families in about three weeks."

It was a bit cooler today. The sea wind fluttered Su Phan's shirt above her black pants as she watched the ships prepare to sail. The wind was a good omen. It would carry the ships swiftly toward the big port. Watching the men scurry back and forth, Su Phan once again imagined what it would be like to be on the ship and drift across the sea with the flying birds and the swimming fish. She wanted to see other places far from her own small village.

But today, a heaviness was in her, a fear that clutched and did not let go. "Papa," she said, clinging to his arm, "Do not leave. Stay here a while longer. Wait until the war is over."

He touched her hair. "Mui, Mui, you know I cannot do that. The war will go on. In the meantime, I must make a living."

As tears welled in her eyes, he said, "Be a good girl. Mind your elders. I will bring you sesame candy as always. And then you shall sing for your father."

The whole family came to watch and wave as the ships set sail. Finally all three vessels disappeared beyond the horizon.

Suddenly Grandmother burst into a fit of weeping. "*Bay la!* My God, my son will not return!"

"He will return," Mother said, but her voice sounded uncertain. As they walked along the dirt path to the house, Su Phan's brother and sister, who usually pushed each other playfully and laughed, now walked silently. Mother said, "Now all we can do is wait and pray."

Each day Grandmother lit incense before Kuan Yin, the Chinese goddess of protection, and prayed for her son's safe return. *Why does she pray so long?* Su Phan wondered. *Didn't Father tell us not to worry?*

Again, the dark fear within her stirred, but not for long. Su Phan convinced herself that all would be well. Her father would sail back soon. She went skipping off to play with Lien and the others. Her clamshell collection was growing because she was very good at tossing the shells near the line but not beyond it.

Suddenly there was a roar overhead, so loud the girls

put their hands over their ears. They looked up to see the sky darkened with airplanes.

"I wish they'd fly somewhere else!" Lien exclaimed. "I hate the noise those planes make!"

Some boys standing nearby hooted with laughter. "Planes? Those are bombers, you stupid girl!" one of them said. "Don't you know there's a war going on?"

"Well, yes. But what has that to do with us?" Lien replied.

"Do with us?" The boy shook his head. To his friends, he said, "Do you believe this?" He looked back at Lien. "Wake up. We've been fighting for years and it'll probably go on forever."

In a school-teacherish kind of way another boy said, "Little girls, you understand that we have to make South Vietnam accept our views on Communism, don't you?"

"We all know that," Su Phan said defensively. She looked at her friends, who gave dubious nods. Actually, they all knew very little, except for the babble at school about their leader, Ho Chi Minh, and how he would lead the Communist troops to victory. She wasn't very interested in the war and they seldom talked about it at home.

An older boy spoke up. "We'd have won long ago if it weren't for the Americans butting in, taking the South's side and bombing us." With a wicked grin he said, "Right now, they're probably getting into their planes to come drop a huge bomb right on our village, maybe on the spot where you're standing!"

Without thinking, Su Phan moved a few feet. Her heart started to race.

Laughing, the boys went on their way, bragging about how the bombers from North Vietnam would wipe out the army of the South.

The girls exchanged glances, their game forgotten.

"Can what they said be true?" Su Phan asked, trembling.

"True enough," Khenh said. "I hear the elders talk and they say the war will grow worse."

"In what way?" Peng asked.

"More bombs will be dropped. More people killed."

"Here?" Su Phan gasped. "In our little village?"

"No, just the big cities," Khenh said. "Unless they drop some on us by mistake. For myself, I don't believe that will happen. But of course, it could." She looked around uneasily.

Su Phan didn't want to hear any more. Leaving her clamshells, she whirled around and ran home crying.

"What is it?" her grandmother asked, turning from the pile of sticks she'd been gathering to take inside for their cooking fire. "What is the matter with you? Have you hurt yourself? I don't see any blood."

"A boy said that bombs fall on villages and kill people! Will they kill us?"

"Such nonsense!" The grandmother snorted. "Those things happen far away and do not concern us. Now be quiet and go help your mother. Try to be useful instead of crying like a baby."

Her mother was hoeing in the vegetable garden. When she saw Su Phan's tear-streaked face she stopped and stared. "What's wrong?"

Su Phan told her about the airplanes and bombs.

"Grandmother said they won't come here. Is that so?"

"Your ah mah is right. The war is far away. There is no need for us to worry." But in spite of her brave words, a look of anxiety came over Mother's face and her eyes closed briefly, as if she were praying.

That evening the family sat around the fire saying little as Mother dished out seafood soup in small bowls. When they'd finished that, she gave them vegetables and rice.

"I heard from the other boys," Senh Hau said, busy with his chopsticks, "that the war is coming closer. Soon we'll be in the middle of it."

"Hush," his mother said. "That is only talk among idle boys. You shouldn't listen to them. You should do your schoolwork so that you will grow up to be smart, like your father."

"I don't want to be a trader," Senh Hau said. "I want to be a soldier, and fight."

"Be quiet!" Grandmother shouted. "I will not listen to talk like this from my own flesh and blood. Shame! You should be beaten with sticks for such blasphemy!"

"I'm only saying . . ." the boy began.

"Hush!" his mother warned. "We will not hear such talk. Your grandmother is right. When your father returns . . ."

"He will beat you," Su Phan said, but only loud enough for her brother to hear.

"When he returns we will find out more about the war," their mother went on. "Until then, we will not discuss it. We know nothing. We are only women and one young boy."

Senh Hau scowled at being called a young boy. At the age of eleven he considered himself almost grown up.

They waited and waited for Father's return. Four weeks went by, then five. Su Phan stood on the shore and watched as before, trembling in spite of the heat. In her nervousness she chewed on the end of one pigtail, wrapped with pink string.

At first her friends stood with her but then they grew tired of watching and went off to play. Even her best friend Lien said, "It's no fun to be around you when you're always so sad."

Su Phan grew lonely. She tried the strings-on-her-fingers game but nothing happened. *Perhaps,* she thought, *if I don't watch, father will surprise me and bring home his ships.*

Still, she had no heart for games with her friends. Finally, one morning, she decided to do something she'd often wanted to do. She'd follow her grandmother as she walked to the market in the next village to buy vegetables and a bit of pork.

She'd always wondered what this big market was like, but her grandmother would never let her tag along. "I am content with my own company," she'd said the last time Su Phan had pestered her about going. "I do not need you bothering me with all your questions."

So this day Su Phan followed at a distance, but then, since Grandmother walked so slowly, she got closer and closer. Suddenly the old woman stopped to rest, turned, and spied her granddaughter. She stood there glaring, and beckoned for the girl to come nearer.

When Su Phan reached her side, Grandmother said, "Come here," and broke a twig from a small tree. "See this switch? You've felt it on your legs often enough when you were little. You think now you are too old to be beaten?" She flicked the switch so hard it made a zinging sound, but Su Phan leaped out of the way.

"Go home! Help your mother! I do not want you dragging along behind me like a dog covered with fleas."

All of her life Su Phan had listened to her grandmother's scolding. Once she had been in awe of her anger but through the years she had come to know it was only talk, as meaningless as water falling over stones.

Su Phan turned and walked away, then looked back when she felt it was safe. Sure enough, Grandmother had resumed her way along the uneven dirt path. Su Phan scurried along behind and then hid in the bushes. She saw the old woman stop and look back again. Finally, satisfied that she had gotten rid of the pesky child, she went on.

They proceeded, with Su Phan hurrying behind, and hiding now and then. When they finally reached the market, the girl followed her grandmother inside the big bamboo shelter. Somehow Su Phan hadn't expected it to be such a large place. She looked at the long rows of booths where people were shouting, "Come see my spices!" "Come buy my fish . . . very fresh!"

Attached to nearly every other post was a huge picture of Ho Chi Minh, who seemed to be looking down at the bustle of the market. Su Phan tried not to meet his stern stare. Their leader did not approve of disobedient children. At least that's what the teachers at school said.

She followed the figure of her grandmother, who was weaving down this aisle and that. The heat of the building was stifling, and the smells of spices, meat, and fish were making Su Phan dizzy.

She paused to look at a huge pyramid of cone hats, some plain and some embroidered with fine designs. How wonderful it would be to own such a treasure! A smiling woman beckoned to the girl and held out a small hat for her to try. Su Phan put it on and the woman said, "Very beautiful. Very cheap. Do you want to buy it?"

"I have no money," Su Phan said. She put back the hat and looked around. Then she panicked. Where was her grandmother? How could she find her among all these twisting aisles? Hurrying, wiping sweat from her face, she went down one line of booths, around the corner, and then up another aisle. Finally she spied her grandmother, leaning over a pile of vegetables, sorting through them to find the freshest.

She rushed forward and stood smiling until her grandmother, picking up a bunch of greens, turned and noticed her.

"So! You are here anyway, after I told you to go back home!"

Su Phan kept on smiling.

Grandmother sighed. "Ah well, as long as you are here I suppose you are hungry." She bought Su Phan a stick of sweet sugarcane to chew on, and a banana.

Munching happily, Su Phan was glad she'd made the trip. She knew that although her grandmother spoke in a stern voice and seldom showed affection, she actually loved her grandchildren very much.

She remembered what her brother Senh Hau had once said. "When Grandmother dies, I will take my blanket to the mountain where she has been placed and I will lie by her grave." Su Phan thought she would probably do the same.

Chapter
4

AS TIME PASSED AND STILL Su Phan's father did not return, Grandmother refused to eat. She sat by the door rocking and moaning, "*Bay la! Bay la!* It is as I have said. We will never see my son Chung Bo again!" And when she saw Su Phan crying, she would say, "It is right to cry, little girl. You will not sing for your father again. He is gone forever."

At these words Su Phan sobbed until her mother came and held her close. "Hush, hush. It is only an old woman's fears. Do not feel sad. It will be all right."

Then one day a fisherman came to the house. "I have heard about your husband," he told Su Phan's mother. "His boats have been seized by the Communist officials."

"Oh no! But what about him?" Voong Nhi Mui cried out. "What has happened to my husband?"

"That I cannot tell you. I do not know."

"Does anyone know?" Mother asked, wringing her hands.

The fisherman shuffled his dusty feet in their black thongs, looked at the family with sympathy in his eyes, and went away.

That evening the family sat on the floor around the fire. Their supper of fish and vegetables bubbled in the pot supported by stones, but no one had any desire for food. Grandmother rocked and moaned without ceasing, tears falling from her eyes.

"Perhaps I will go and find our father," Su Phan's brother said.

"Be quiet," Mother commanded. "You cannot walk for many miles and seek him out. Where would you look? Perhaps he is even in jail."

At this, the girls began to wail.

"Hush," Mother said. "Crying will not bring back your father."

"But what can we do?" Su Phan sobbed, leaning on her elbows, hands covering her eyes.

"There is nothing we can do but wait," Mother said. "And pray."

Many days and nights passed. Then one evening, just as they were lighting incense and praying before the statue of Kuan Yin, the door suddenly opened and there stood Chung Bo.

"Father!" the children shouted.

"My husband!" their mother cried out, unbelieving.

"My son! My son has returned!" Grandmother wailed. "May the heavens be praised!"

Chung Bo embraced each member of his family and then sank with great weariness onto a small stool near the fire.

"What happened? Where have you been?" the children wanted to know.

"Be still," their mother said. "First your father must eat and rest. Then he will tell us about his journey."

Su Phan had never seen her strong father look so weary. His shirt, usually clean and fresh looking, was dingy and torn, perhaps from thorny bushes. His black cotton pants were torn, too, and there were ugly red scratches along his legs.

He said he was very hungry, but when Mother put food in front of him he was too tired to swallow more than half a bowl of rice.

"The Communist authorities seized my ships," he finally said, his hand brushing his forehead as though to collect his thoughts.

"So we have heard," Mother said. "But then how did you get back to us?"

"Fortunately for me and the others, the South Vietnamese and the Americans bombed near the place where we were being held. In the confusion, we managed to escape."

"But how did you make your way home?" Su Phan's brother asked.

"By walking at night and hiding during the day. We crossed mountains and struggled through forests." Chung Bo bent back and forward to ease the soreness of his back. "At last, three of my men and I found a fisherman who was willing to bring us the rest of the way for the money we had managed to hide in our clothing." He passed his hand across his forehead again. "Now I am tired, so tired."

"Rest, my son," Grandmother said.

"Yes," his wife agreed. "Sleep is what you need now. There will be plenty of time later to think about getting new ships."

"New ships?" Chung Bo said sharply. "What would be the use of that? The authorities would only take them as well. While they were holding us they made it very clear that they will no longer tolerate independent boat trade."

"Then, Father, what will you do?" his son asked.

"I thought much about that on the long way home. I will build a store. If I cannot take my goods to people, the people will have to come to me."

Su Phan felt happy when she heard those words. Her father would not go away again. He would stay with them always and they would be happy all the time.

Chapter
5

"SU PHAN, YOU ARE LUCKY to have such a rich father," her friend Lien said. They were standing outside near the road, watching men put the finishing touches on the new store. They had already built a second story on the house where the family would now sleep. The large sleeping room downstairs was being converted into the store, with counters and shelves.

Su Phan had never thought of her family as rich, but she supposed her friend was right. Su Phan's mother had been just a child, and so had her father, when their families left China for Vietnam. They grew up, married, and in due time inherited the family treasures.

Among these treasures were chopsticks made of ivory, and beautiful gold jewelry that now belonged to Su Phan's mother. She seldom wore this jewelry, though. It was hidden away in a big Chinese chest, upstairs in the sleeping quarters.

The family dressed in the Vietnamese style, but their clothes were made from a softer, finer cotton. Folded away in the large chest, carefully wrapped in rice paper, there were also Chinese garments of thick, richly embroidered silk. Su Phan's parents sometimes took out these robes, put them on for a special occasion, then carefully refolded them and put them away again.

Once, on a fine summer day, when everyone was gone from the house except Su Phan and her sister, Su Lenh, they decided to open the forbidden chest and look at the embroidered silk finery.

"What will happen if Mother and Father come back and find we have opened the chest and taken out these things?" Su Phan asked, tracing the lines of the brilliant dragon on the back of a red robe.

"You baby," her sister replied. "They have gone far away to visit the temple and will not be back until evening. I'm going to put this on, this fine green robe."

Su Phan gasped. "You wouldn't dare!"

"Oh, yes, I would." Su Lenh was already slipping her slender arms through the sleeves. She pulled the front together and fastened it. "How do I look, Su Phan?" She turned, took a few steps, and gracefully turned around again. She lifted her long, dark hair, never cut since the time she was one month old, twisted it into a knot, and posed. "Am I beautiful?" she asked.

Su Phan wished she were as tall as her sister and that her own hair had grown farther down, far past her shoulders. "You look foolish, trying to be grown up," the smaller girl said. She didn't want to admit that her sister looked beautiful. Su Lenh's face had taken on a soft glow from the reflection of the silken fabric. "And besides, the gown is much too long for you."

"I know it's too long, little cabbage." Su Lenh took hold of the sides of the robe and lifted them. Then she gave a little gasp. "Oh, no! I've dragged the hem across the floor and now look at the dirty smudges!"

Su Phan knelt and examined the lower edges of the gown. "What should we do? Wash them off?"

"Stupid! One does not wash garments such as these." "Then what we must do," Su Phan said, "is fold the robe as we found it and put it back. By the time it's discovered we'll have thought of something." She was proud of herself for being so sensible when her sister, older but not wiser, had no notion of how to deal with a problem.

Standing here now with Lien, watching the men working on the store, Su Phan thought again of the soiled robe. It would not be long before a Chinese festival day arrived. Her parents would open the chest, take out the silk garments, and then what? Su Phan had felt a switch in the past, but had never been beaten. She was afraid that she would be this time.

"Why don't we go inside the store?" Lien asked. "And then up on the roof? Don't say it's impossible because I saw you up there myself."

Su Phan hesitated for a moment, then shrugged and led the way. She'd wanted to keep the high-up place to herself, a little retreat where she could gaze at the sea and dream. But she was afraid that if she said this to Lien, her friend would laugh.

Su Phan led the way through the nearly finished store, with its shelves ready to hold folded lengths of fabric, and the fine counter, made from planks of wood supported by bamboo trestles. At first, before the upstairs had been completed, the family had lived in the back. But now that area was used for storage, as well as for family cooking and eating.

Steps led to the second floor where the family slept, and where the Chinese trunk was kept. In a corner Father had built an altar for Kuan Yin. Around the figure of the goddess were pots for incense and painted Chinese vases that held flowers on festival days.

Su Phan, followed by her friend, then climbed a small ladder and pushed a doorlike covering that let them out to the thatched roof. "Be careful to step on the boards, so you don't fall through," Su Phan warned.

"Oh, it's so high!" Lien exclaimed. "It's like being on top of the world."

"You can see far out across the water," Su Phan said, standing at the front of the roof.

"Look at the ships!" Lien pointed at distant sails.

"That black one coming in looks like a mother duck," Su Phan said, "and the ones behind her, like little ducklings." But as she said this, she became very sad. Here she had a fine view of the sea, but never again would she see her father's ships coming in.

"I wish," she said to Lien, "that I could have come up here before my father's ships were taken."

"But," the practical girl pointed out, "if he still went out to sea, you wouldn't have this store that is also your home."

Su Phan wondered if life was always this way . . . that you must give up one thing in order to have something new.

Chapter
6

A FEW DAYS LATER THE STORE was entirely finished and Su Phan's father began gathering more goods to sell.

"You, Senh Hau," he said to his son, "will be in charge of the store while I am out getting merchandise. Be sure you handle the money well. I will insist on an exact account when I return."

"You can depend on me," Senh Hau said. "I am very good at math, if you remember."

"I forget nothing. For instance, that you and your sisters will soon be returning to school. But in the meantime, take care of everything here during my absence."

Senh Hau loved being in charge of the store. He felt he was in charge of his sisters, as well.

"Go fetch the broom," he said to Su Lenh, "and sweep the floor properly." To Su Phan he said, "I do not like the arrangement of the sticks of incense. Please line them up in better order."

When the girls objected to his bossing them around, Senh Hau folded his arms and scowled. "Remember, I am in charge here and my orders are to be obeyed. If you don't do as I say, I'll report your disobedience to our father."

"Go ahead," Su Phan said, making a face at her brother. "I'll tell him how mean and bossy you are."

"And I'll tell how you took some sweets for yourself and didn't give us any," the older sister said.

"Enough!" Senh Hau shouted. "Get to work!"

"Or what?" Su Phan retorted. Nevertheless she went over to the counter and began to arrange the incense sticks in little pyramids. She had just finished with the last bunch when a roar overhead startled her so much that her hand knocked over the pile.

"Those must be planes—American planes!" Senh Hau said. "Ours don't fly so low. I'll go have a look at them!"

"No!" Su Phan shouted, grabbing his leg. "Don't go out there. You might get hurt!"

"Stupid! They're not interested in bombing a small village like ours. They must be heading farther north."

"Please stay with us! I'm afraid!" Su Lenh cried, holding on to him as well.

"Babies, both of you," Senh Hau grumbled, but as the roaring planes grew louder still, he pushed them to the floor and crouched beside them.

Suddenly there was a whooshing sound, followed by a horrendous bang. "They *are* dropping bombs!" Senh Hau said in a voice now quivering with fear. "Oh, Mother . . . I hope you are still at the well and far from all this!"

"What's that terrible racket?"

They looked around to see their grandmother stumbling down the steps toward them. The bomb had aroused her from her nap.

"Get down, Grandmother!" Su Lenh screamed, pulling at the old woman. "They're dropping bombs! We're going to be killed!"

"Don't yell!" Su Phan said, although she herself was shouting. "Be quiet so the bombs can't find us!"

With contempt, Senh Hau said, "The airplanes can't hear *us*. But be quiet, anyway. All of you."

And then as quickly as the noise had started, it stopped. The roar of the airplanes grew fainter and finally faded into the distance.

"It's safe now, I think," Senh Hau said, getting up and helping his ah mah to her feet. "That noise we heard was just to put fear into the village. But of course I was not afraid."

"Then why . . ." Su Phan started to say, but screams from outside kept her from finishing the question.

"What? What?" Grandmother exclaimed. The children had no answers. Leaving the old woman behind they ran out of the store toward the spot where a crowd was gathering.

"Don't look!" An older woman said, pushing them back.

"What happened?" Senh Hau asked.

"Never mind. Just go back to your home."

Reluctantly, they backed up, still trying to look beyond the crowd. But the excited people, cone hats bobbing, blocked out the view.

A young boy came running up to them. "Did you see it?"

"What?"

"Where the bomb fell. It made a big hole in the path over there. And you know what else?"

Su Phan huddled behind her brother, wanting to hear, and yet afraid.

"It blew an old woman all to bits! You can see pieces . . ."

"Be quiet!" Senh Hau said. And to his sisters, "Go into the house."

The girls ran. Inside the store their grandmother asked, "Well, what was it?"

Su Lenh started to tell, but Su Phan ran upstairs and hid under the sweet grass mat that covered her bed.

Maybe the bomb had been a mistake. People said their village was safe. But was it? She continued to huddle under the mat until she finally heard her mother's voice. Then she crept downstairs.

"Don't be afraid, my children," Mother said, setting down two full buckets of water. "What happened today won't happen again. Soon your father will be home and we'll all be safe."

How could her mother know for sure? Su Phan wondered. Perhaps words couldn't always be believed, even when they came from a parent.

She'd be glad when her father returned, but would she be safe? Father was a strong and wise man, but how could he protect them against a death that dropped suddenly from the sky?

Chapter 7

WHEN CHUNG BO RETURNED a few days later, people were still talking about the bomb. The woman who had been killed, they said, was walking along the path with a basket of cabbages. "She had only a few moments of warning, not enough time to flee," they said.

"I heard about it along the way," Chung Bo said. "It's a very bad thing. But most people believe the bomb fell from the American plane by mistake. It is not likely to happen again."

"Still," Su Phan said, "perhaps we shouldn't go to school next week when it opens. Just to be on the safe side."

The frown that had creased her father's face disappeared as he smiled. "Mui, Mui, you will not get off going so easily. Of course you'll return to school. It's important that you study and learn."

"But she is only a girl," Grandmother said, setting down

her teacup. "Why does she need to go to school? The lessons she should learn are how to cook and clean."

"Quiet," Chung Bo commanded. "I want all of my children to know how to read and do arithmetic. In our family learning is important—for girls as well as boys."

Grandmother shuffled off mumbling, but she said no more on the subject.

Chung Bo's store was not as well supplied as his ships had been. He had no trouble getting workers to make incense, but securing fabrics was difficult. Bribes had to be paid, along with high taxes. And now it was against the law to sell sake, even though it was as popular a drink as ever. Chung Bo didn't want to take the risk of secretly supplying it to customers.

"Father," Senh Hau said, "what will you do? How can you make as much money as before?"

"I can't," Chung Bo said. "However, we'll sell cookies and sweet treats, which the women of the house will prepare. And I have arranged for people from far-off villages to bring large amounts of sugar and rice. Perhaps we won't make as much money as before, but we will still be better off than most."

School started despite the war, and all three children trudged off to the schoolhouse, several miles away. They carried their lunches in tall containers called *cap longs*. Each one held vegetables in the upper tray and steamed rice in the one below.

Senh Hau walked swiftly with his friends, and Su Lenh followed with hers. Su Phan dawdled along the way with Lien, Khenh, and Peng. Often one of the girls would run ahead of the others, hide in the shrubbery, and then leap out. Because of their antics, they sometimes got to school just as the bell was ringing.

On these occasions, Su Lenh scolded her sister. "One of these days you are going to be late for school, and then you'll be punished," she said.

"No, I won't," Su Phan replied.

"And when Father finds out, he will punish you some more," Su Lenh went on.

"No, he won't," Su Phan repeated.

"You think not? Just because you're the youngest doesn't mean that you can do whatever you like. You're not a baby anymore, even though you sometimes act like one."

Su Phan sulked, but still she heeded her sister's words. She didn't want to be considered a baby. The next time her friends started the hiding game, she said in a lofty manner, "I wish you would stop acting so silly. We're not little children, you know."

"Oh, listen to her," Peng said. "Su Phan is trying to be grown up."

"Su Phan, you needn't put on airs just because your father is so rich," Khenh added.

"My father is not rich," Su Phan said. And she thought, *Not rich at all, considering my ancestors.* She had never told her friends that her great-great-great-grandparents had lived in the court of the Chinese emperor.

"Su Phan is not putting on airs," Lien said loyally. "Is

it her fault that the gods have been good to her family?"

The other girls sniffed but said nothing.

At times like this, Su Phan was embarrassed by her family's good fortune, for she herself had done nothing to deserve it.

Chapter 8

SU PHAN LOVED TO HELP in her father's store after school. It seemed so grand to her, compared to the other village shops that were little more than workrooms with bits of merchandise sitting on mats outside. People had to go from shop to shop to look for what they needed.

"We have such a fine place!" she exclaimed one day to her father as she touched the fabrics lying folded on the shelves. "Better by far than any other store."

Chung Bo smiled. "It may be finer than the other shops here, but it's poor compared to the stores in large cities. Till now you have seen only this small village— such a small place that the streets aren't even named."

Su Phan laughed. "Why would people want to name their streets?"

"So they can get directions for where they want to go. When streets have names they are easier to find." Father smiled as he visualized the scene. "Some people in cities walk to where they are going, others pedal their way on bicycles. But many drive motorbikes with sidecars that can carry a whole family."

Su Phan couldn't imagine such a place. "I'd like to see a city like that."

"When this war is over, Mui, I will take you there," her father said, smoothing her hair.

But as each day passed, the dangers of the present drove away Su Phan's daydreams. Customers coming into the store brought stories they had heard from travelers passing through, or even from North Vietnamese soldiers on the march.

"Have you heard?" someone would ask. "They have bombed a village just to the north, not so very far away. We could be bombed ourselves any day now."

"Father," Su Phan said one day, after the last customer had gone and her father was fastening the wooden door across the entrance, "will the war really find us here?"

"Mui," he answered gruffly, "you should not stand around in the store listening to grown-up talk. Go upstairs and do your schoolwork."

Upstairs, Su Lenh was already hard at work on her studies.

"Sister," Su Phan said, "are you afraid that when the planes fly overhead they will drop bombs on us?"

"I don't let myself think of it, and you shouldn't, either." But then Su Lenh looked up, and realizing that Su Phan was terribly frightened, she softened her tone. "We're safe enough here," she said. "Our father himself has said so, and he's older and wiser than we are. Instead of bad thoughts, why don't you fill your mind with the stories Father used to tell us when we were little? Try to dream of dragons."

Su Phan shook her head. "I'm afraid to dream of dragons."

"Oh, and why is that?"

"Because they spit out fiery breath and kill anyone who comes near them. They're like the monster airplanes that rain fire from the sky."

Su Lenh sighed heavily. "What is one to do with such a silly girl? Really, Su Phan, your thoughts are much too fanciful. Settle down and put your mind on school and the work you have to do. You'll never be a Ho Chi Minh honor student like your brother and me unless you study harder."

Perhaps my sister is right, Su Phan thought. No one else in the family seemed to think they were in danger. Her brother and his friends often ran outside when bombers flew over. They darted around and shouted at them, and tried to guess whose planes they were, the North's or the South's. Often the bombers were too high in the sky to tell.

That night it was quiet and Su Phan forgot her fears. The family sat around the fire as usual for their evening meal. Then they went upstairs and her father lit his pipe and said, as he often did, "Mui, Mui, come sing for your father." She sang the new song she had learned at school that day.

Suddenly, when she was in the middle of the second verse, her mother touched her arm and said, "Hush. What was that? I heard a noise downstairs, outside the door."

Chung Bo put his pipe aside and listened.

"Is it thieves, come to rob the store?" Senh Hau whispered.

But then there was a loud, crashing sound as though the door to the store was being kicked open. Thieves wouldn't make such a loud noise. As Chung Bo went toward the steps, voices started shouting, "Where is he? Where is this Chung Bo?"

Terrified, the family clustered around Chung Bo. "Let's hide," Su Phan said fearfully.

"There is no place to hide," he said. "I'll go down and see what this is all about." He shrugged off his wife's arms and started down the stairs.

"There he is!" a voice shouted. "Grab the merchant!"

Voong Nhi Mui, who was close behind her husband, screamed. Su Phan, peering fearfully down the stairs, saw a soldier grab her father and throw him to the floor.

"Stay back!" he shouted over his shoulder to the family, but Senh Hau rushed downstairs. He, too, was seized and thrown to the floor.

From the steps, Grandmother wailed and Mother sobbed as they watched the military police swarm through the store. The policemen wore yellow uniforms and caps and carried long guns. While Su Phan watched, they broke open containers and spilled the contents on the floor.

Then Father was pulled to his feet and his wrists were tied with a rope. The policemen dragged him toward the door, which was now hanging loose.

"So you think you're too good to be a Communist, eh?" shouted one soldier, delivering a kick. "Well, we'll soon fix that. Take him away!"

"Let go of him!" Senh Hau screamed. A soldier swung around and hit Senh Hau on the side of the head with his rifle. The cut began to bleed.

Su Phan pushed past her mother and ran down the stairs to where her brother lay. "You've hurt him! You're mean, mean, mean!" she screamed.

"Be quiet, Su Phan," her brother said, wiping blood from his cheek with his sleeve.

While some of the policemen continued to destroy the merchandise in the store, others rushed past the women on the stairs. Su Phan heard crashing and banging overhead, and the sound of dishes breaking. Then the soldiers came back down carrying money, jewelry, and precious objects made of ivory.

One soldier had the beautiful green Chinese robe— the one Su Lenh had tried on—hanging from his gun. As he waved it around, laughing, Su Phan saw it had been ripped. Now the soldier threw it on the floor and stomped on it with his dirty boots.

"Let's go!" the leader said. "Put that stuff in the truck, you two, and the rest of you take this Chinese scum away."

"But what has my husband done?" Voong Nhi Mui wailed as Chung Bo was dragged out the door by the rope around his wrists. "What has he done?"

"It's what he has not done," the leader shouted. "He has not become a Communist, as everyone should. It's wrong for one person to have so much when others have so little. We'll keep him in prison until he learns the ways of Communism."

"When will you let him return?" Mother cried out.

"In two or three years, if he learns his lessons well," the policeman answered. "And now be quiet, all of you!"

But the women screamed as they rushed to the door to see Chung Bo shoved into the back of a truck. Senh Hau shook his fist as the truck rumbled away. "You won't get away with this!" he shouted.

"Don't . . ." Su Phan begged. She was afraid the soldiers would hear and come back for her brother as well.

Grandmother sat on the floor, put her face in her hands, and began swaying and moaning. "*Bay la!* They will kill him! We will never see Chung Bo again!"

"Hush," Mother said as she stood staring at the empty street.

Su Lenh spoke softly to her brother. "I'll bathe your face," she said. She went upstairs to get a bowl of water, but the water jar had been spilled and all the dishes had been broken.

Now neighbors began coming quietly to the door and peering inside.

"What are you staring at?" Su Lenh screamed. "Have you come to rejoice at our disaster?"

"We mean only to help," a woman said.

"Then go fetch me a bowl and some water and some cloths!" Su Lenh commanded. "Can't you see that my brother is injured?"

The children didn't go to school the next day. Instead, they swept up the spilled rice and sugar, dirty now and not fit to eat. The beautiful pieces of fabric were torn and ruined, and the Chinese robe was a mass of ripped cloth.

43

Still, Su Phan folded it carefully and put it aside. "Perhaps some day I can mend this robe," she said, "and make the dragon whole again."

Upstairs, she saw that Grandmother still sat before what was once the altar, now completely destroyed. Over and over she picked up pieces of the shattered lady god and tried to put them together. Moaning sounds came from deep in her throat.

"Come, lie down," Su Phan coaxed, but the old woman seemed not to hear. Finally, giving up, Su Phan went back to her mother and tried to get her to drink the hot tea a neighbor had brought.

Mother would have none of it, nor would she stir from the woven mat another neighbor had given them, to replace the one that was ruined. "Let me die!" she moaned. "Let me die so I may be with my husband!"

Then Su Phan began to sob. Turning to her sister, she asked, "Is he dead? Is our father dead?"

"Hush," Su Lenh said. "You mustn't carry on this way. Make yourself useful. Go help Senh Hau with the cleaning up."

Obediently, Su Phan trudged downstairs. Her brother, in his father's absence, was now the man of the house, and his sisters had to obey him.

But still he looked very young, and pale. His head was bandaged and there was a swelling under one eye.

"Does it hurt a lot, your head?" Su Phan asked.

"A little. But it is nothing compared to the suffering of our father."

Su Phan bit her lip to keep from crying.

"Don't be afraid, Mui," her brother said in a new, gentle voice. "I will take care of everything until he returns."

"Then . . . they will not kill him?"

"No!" her brother said. "They wouldn't dare! Remember this, Su Phan. He is still Chung Bo, the trader, a man of importance."

She nodded, comforted. But later, lying in bed, she saw once again her father being dragged from the house, tied with ropes like an animal. She cried, but quietly, so the others wouldn't hear.

And then, to make that scene go away from her mind, she tried to remember the sound of Chung Bo's voice as he said, "Mui, Mui, come sing for your father."

She began to sing, moving her lips but not making a sound.

Chapter
9

"I HATE THOSE COMMUNISTS!" Su Phan said, kicking a clump of dirt. "Hate them, hate them, hate them!"

"Don't," her friend Lien gasped, grabbing Su Phan's arm and looking around anxiously. They were on their way to school and, as usual, the four friends were walking together.

Khenh and Peng whirled around in front of Su Phan, stopping her. "You mustn't say things like that," Khenh cautioned, nervously glancing at other students walking along the path. "It's not safe. What if someone heard you?"

"What if they did? I don't care," Su Phan said. "It's what I think. The Communists are mean and spiteful. They took away my father just because . . ." Actually, she wasn't sure why they had.

"Because he used to be friendly to the French," Peng said.

"No, it's because he made too much money with his independent business," Khenh said.

"My parents said it was because he refused to become a Communist," Lien added.

"So! You're all against my father . . . against me!" Su Phan tried to push past her friends but they wouldn't budge.

"Calm down. We're only telling you what people are saying. It's talk, nothing else. But you might as well get used to it," Khenh said.

Lien picked up the cap long that Su Phan had dropped. "You should just remember, no matter what people say, that your father was a good man. Didn't he sometimes give us treats when we went into the store? Didn't he laugh and tease?"

"That's right," the others said, nodding. "He was good, your father."

"But still," Khenh couldn't help adding, "it would be better if he had been Communist like all the rest of the village."

Su Phan gave her a look as she walked on. "People spied on us. They were jealous. That's what my sister says, and I think she's right."

"Where *is* Su Lenh?" Lien asked. "Isn't she going to school today?"

"No. She is staying home to look after my mother and grandmother. They're sick with grieving for my father." Su Phan sighed. "I wish I could be there, too."

Su Phan wished even more that she had stayed home when she reached the school yard. Students stood in clumps, talking. When they turned and saw Su Phan

47

their heads bobbed together in such a way that she knew they were talking about her.

Then at a little distance Su Phan heard loud voices. A group of boys had surrounded her brother, Senh Hau, and were chanting, "Chung Bo di tu ba nam chua ve!" *Your father is in prison for three years and will not come back!*

"Stop that, you insect-brains!" Su Phan shouted, dashing over to the boys. They only laughed, shoved her aside, and chanted even louder.

"Go away," Senh Hau mumbled to his sister, looking embarrassed. It was bad enough to be taunted, but to have a girl, and his younger sister at that, try to come to his rescue!

The school bell sounded, and the children, suddenly quiet, walked inside in an orderly fashion.

Is this the way it will be now? Su Phan wondered. *Everyone against our family?* Even her friends stayed just a little apart, as though it was better not to seem too close.

As usual, the school day began with the song about Communism, but Su Phan could not sing. Looking up at the picture of Uncle Ho, she wondered if he was quite so wonderful as everyone said. Would he approve of what the military police had done to her father? If so, he wasn't kind at all.

The school day dragged on, as did the days that followed. In time Su Phan and her brother grew used to the taunts of their classmates and were no longer angered by them. It was their life. And if their friends avoided them at school, they knew it was only to keep from being jeered at themselves. Back in the neighborhood they continued to play together as before.

At home, life was totally changed. The carefree, prosperous times were over. Now Su Phan's family, having lost everything, was poorer than the poor.

One night Su Lenh asked when she might go back to school.

Her mother sadly shook her head. "I am afraid you will have to stay home all the time now and help your grandmother. I will have to go out and work to bring in some money."

"What about me?" Senh Hau asked. "I'm big and strong. I'll find work, too."

"No, son. I want you to stay in school. Learn all you can. It is what your father would wish."

Senh Hau scowled. "Father's in prison. So we should do as *we* wish, and not follow his commands."

"Shame! Shame!" Mother shouted. Her face was red with fury and she raised her hand as if to strike him, but Senh Hau backed away. "Your father is still head of the house!" she said. " We will always do as he wished! You understand?"

Su Phan, who had almost offered to stay home, too, kept silent. She knew her grandmother would make her work very hard and yet complain about how she did the chores. It was much better to be off with her friends all day, even if school life wasn't all that pleasant anymore.

Soon Mother was going off to work each day before the sun brought full light. She had been able to find hard labor, shoveling stones for the laying of train tracks the army was putting down near the village. Each night she came home bone weary, hardly able to lift her head to eat.

"Mother," Su Phan said one night, grasping her mother's hands. "They're all blistered. This work is too hard for you."

"Soon they'll be calloused," Mother said, drawing away her hands. "And I won't feel anything then."

"But it's too much!" Su Phan said, starting to cry.

In former days her mother would have drawn her daughter close and comforted her. But she was growing colder. "It is nothing compared to the suffering of your father," she said. "Now, leave me alone, and stop your crying and complaining. You're too big to cry."

It seemed to Su Phan that all the beauty and happiness of her former life had disappeared. The nice things in her home were gone, and their house was simply a shell.

The door to the store still hung open where it had been broken. "Leave it," Mother said one day when Senh Hau tried to repair the door. "We have nothing left for anyone to steal." Even the mosquitoes seemed to know that they could now come into the house whenever they wanted. At first they tormented Su Phan with their buzzing and their bites. But soon she stopped paying attention.

What she missed more than anything else was the happy atmosphere that had departed with her father. There was no longer any carefree talk as they squatted on the floor around the cooking pot for their meals. What was there to talk about? Every day was the same as the one before. Except their mother looked more tired and worn each day. As she wearily put food into her mouth she seemed not to notice it was now only rice with a few vegetables from their garden.

Yes, life had changed, and not only within her family. It seemed to Su Phan that the atmosphere of the whole village was different. People who used to laugh and gossip now went about with solemn faces. It was as if a gray cloud had descended upon them all.

Even her sister Su Lenh, weary from housework and gardening, had little to say when they lay in bed at night before going to sleep.

Su Phan felt sad and alone and older. Her father had gone away, and Mui, the little girl who used to sing for him, had vanished as well.

Chapter 10

WAR WAS NOW THE MAIN TOPIC when people gathered to talk.

"The village where my brother lives was bombed by the Americans last week," Su Phan heard a man say as she paused at one of the vegetable stalls near her home. "His family was spared, but many people were killed."

"So I have heard," said a woman carrying a market basket. "Men, women, children, all wiped out. And they say it will get worse before . . ."

Su Phan, clutching her cap long and her books, started walking toward school. She hardly noticed when Lien came up beside her.

"What's the matter?" her friend asked. "Your face is all flushed. Has something happened?" And then she added, "Slow down."

Su Phan stopped, took a deep breath and said, "Have you heard?"

"Heard what?"

"Bombs have fallen on a village not too far away." She wet her lips. "It's not like the one that fell here that time. This was a lot of bombs. Many men, women, and children were killed."

"Oh, everyone knows about that," Lien said. "But what do you expect? We're in a war."

Su Phan started walking rapidly. "How can you be so cold? Don't you care about people?"

"Of course. But what can I do about these things? It's best not to think about them."

Su Phan said no more, but she felt a bit resentful. Lien had her whole family around her, protecting her. Nothing in her life had changed that much.

At school, having no special worries, Lien could do well with her studies. Teachers approved of her. Just this year they had awarded Lien the red tie to wear on her white blouse. This showed she was a fine student, and obedient. It made her one of Ho Chi Minh's children.

Su Phan was certain she would never earn the right to wear the red tie. For one thing, she had to hurry home after school instead of staying and helping the teacher. For another thing, she was said not to be serious. But was it her fault if she giggled, seeing a bug crawl along the teacher's sleeve? Most of all, she did not have a reverent enough attitude when it came to political studies. Once she was almost caught as she mumbled the word *dirty* in front of *Communist*.

In the school yard that day the two girls saw Khenh

53

and Peng as always, and soon it was time to enter the school. It looked the same as always, with sunlight pouring through the wall openings and highlighting bits of straw sifting down from the thatched roof. Students filed in in orderly fashion and sat on the planks of wood that served as benches.

After the opening song and a salute to the nation's leader, Su Phan fitted her pen nib into its wooden holder and dipped it into the ink. Supplies had become scarce during the war, so the ink was watered down to make it go further. The paper was rough and tan-colored, and it was difficult to write on.

The morning droned on. Su Phan's group was doing math when suddenly a shrill sound pierced the air. Students and teachers alike froze for a moment. Could it be that the siren, which had been blown at the beginning of the year just so they would recognize the sound, was now blasting in earnest?

The startled teacher recovered and said, "Children, that was an air raid warning. There is no cause for alarm. It only means that bombers are approaching."

"Bombers!" the children shrilled.

"Don't be alarmed. The airplanes are probably only flying by on their way somewhere else. Still, we will walk quietly to the jungle and stay there until the planes have passed over us."

There was much jostling and arguing as the students charged toward the door. Su Phan felt stiff with fear and unable to move until the teacher turned to her and said, "Well, Su Phan, are you staying?"

Su Phan got up and made her way to the door. The

teacher ushered her out and then hurried after the others.

"Calm down!" she shouted above the noise. "There's time. Don't knock each other down!"

Outside, Su Phan raced with the others toward the jungle, not far from the school.

Some of the boys looked with disdain at the smaller ones who were clinging together and whimpering. Still, they and even the teachers looked solemn and fearful as the terrible sound of the bombers came nearer and nearer.

Su Phan began to tremble. Holding her hands over her face, she whispered over and over, "Please don't let the bombs find us."

It wasn't long before the planes were right overhead. Although they were high up in the sky, their sound vibrated loudly all the way down to the ground. They flew on by, the noise growing fainter until finally it was gone altogether.

The siren sounded again.

"That's the *all clear* signal," one of the teachers said. "We can go back now."

All the students were talking at once as they filed back to the classroom.

One of the boys behind Su Phan said, "I wonder if those were B-52 bombers. They're the worst."

"American?" she asked.

"Of course, American. One of these days, though, we'll shoot them all down, and then the war will be over."

"Meanwhile, I guess we'll be running to the jungle and hiding every time they decide to fly over," another boy said. "What a joke. The Americans can't be interested in bombing a little place like this."

"Be quiet," a girl named Kim Lei said. "The planes got us out of class, didn't they? I hope they come by every day."

The others agreed. Now that the danger was over they were feeling very brave, and happy to have this break in the daily routine.

As the weeks passed the siren sounded more often. It became a part of almost every school day to go into the jungle and hide. No one rushed to get there anymore; instead, they laughed and teased along the way.

One day the planes flew overhead as usual. Thinking little of it, the students were playing around in the jungle when suddenly there came a sound Su Phan had heard once before. The planes had already passed by, but the noise was still loud and chilling, vibrating the very air around them. A moment later there was the blast of an explosion, and then another.

Su Phan spied her brother a short distance away and ran to him. "Senh Hau, I'm so scared!" She buried her face in his chest.

"Hush. It's all right," he said, but there was a tremble in his voice. They listened and heard two more bombs falling from the sky. Then the sound of the airplanes became fainter and finally died away.

The *all clear* sounded. The children filed back into the school, but there was no laughing and talking now.

"Where do you think the bombs fell?" they asked their teacher, who had stood at the door briefly, talking with other teachers.

"Probably beyond the village," she said. "But school is dismissed for the day. You may go home to be with your families."

All the way back Su Phan walked behind her brother. She didn't dare walk with him, because his friends would laugh. But she needed to be near him, at least.

"Ah mah," she cried, upon seeing her grandmother outside the house. "Are you all right?"

"Why wouldn't I be all right?" the old lady asked in her usual abrupt manner. Still, her eyes lingered on her grandchildren before she turned away. And she was mumbling something that sounded like a prayer of thanks.

Chapter
11

When their mother came home that night she rushed to embrace her children. "I worried about you all day," she said. "I didn't know where the other bombs had fallen. One dropped not far from where I was working. It ruined some of the railroad track."

The children begged their mother not to return to work the next day.

"I must," she said. "We need money for rice. Besides, that place may not be bombed again. Destruction can happen anywhere."

"I hate this war!" Su Phan shouted. "Hate it, hate it!"

"Keep that child quiet," Grandmother growled. "She makes more noise than the bombs." And then she added, "Thank goodness I won't have to listen to her much longer. I am moving away."

They all stared at her, too shocked to speak.

"Well, why shouldn't I move away?" the old woman

mumbled as she poked at the fire. "My son is not here. I will go away with my friends to a safer place. A place where I won't have to listen to noisy children."

Su Phan started toward her grandmother to beg her to stay, but her mother grabbed her arm. "Leave her be," she said quietly. "Your ah mah is just talking."

Later that night, unable to sleep, Su Phan heard her grandmother and mother talking downstairs. At first the words were inaudible, but finally, raising her voice, the old woman said, "Do as you please, then. I have already made up my mind."

Su Phan shook her sister. "Wake up, Su Lenh. Grandmother is telling Mother she is really going to leave us."

"Oh, be quiet and go to sleep," Su Lenh said. "It won't happen, believe me."

But the next day when Su Phan came home from school, her grandmother was gone. "Where is she? Where is she?" she cried out to her sister.

"Ah mah, her friend, and her friend's son went off in a boat. She was carrying a bundle of her belongings. I don't know where they were going."

"How could you let her leave?" Su Phan shrieked.

"How could I stop her? She is old and we must respect her wishes."

Su Phan glared at her sister. "You're so weak. If I had been here I would not have let her go!"

Su Lenh gave Su Phan a look of disgust before turning her back.

The younger girl knew she should stay and help her sister, but she was too angry. She ran to where her friends were playing hopscotch.

"What's the matter?" Lien asked.

"Ah mah has gone away. If I had known she was going today I would have stopped her. Or gone along with her, wherever she went."

"Well, too bad," Khenh said. "There's nothing to do now."

"Oh, yes there is. I'll go find her and bring her back."

An older girl had joined the group. "I heard where she went. It's deep in the jungle."

"How deep?" Su Phan asked.

"Very far by land," the girl said, "but not far by boat." With a stick she drew a map in the dirt. "By land you have to go this way and then this way. The path is twisted and it would take at least three hours to get to the place." She looked seriously at Su Phan. "You must cross dangerous jungle bridges, too. I wouldn't try to go there if I were you."

But Su Phan had already decided she would make the trip the very next day. Although it was Saturday, her mother would still go to work. And her brother and sister would rise early to walk the long distance to the well with poles and buckets. With everyone out of the house, it would be easier to slip away.

When she saw her ah mah she would tell her that she was so sad at her leaving that she probably would get ill, very ill, and would no longer be able to attend school. Surely, if she cried just a little, her grandmother's heart would soften and she'd come back to live with the family.

Chapter 12

AT FIRST IT WAS NOT DIFFICULT for Su Phan to find her way. Then she reached the edge of the jungle and the path became narrow and crooked. Every once in a while she had to cross a small bridge of wooden planks. But then she came to a small river and stopped. Here, the bridge was made of bamboo strips joined together.

Su Phan looked at the long, narrow bridge and then down at the water below. The river flowed swiftly, tossing foamy waves over the boulders along the edges.

Did she have the courage to cross this expanse? She took a few steps onto the bamboo flooring. It swayed giddily beneath her feet. There was no handrail, nothing to cling to. Should she go on? Did she dare?

She took a few more steps, trying not to look at the river raging below. Now the swaying increased. Finally she dropped to her hands and knees and crawled from one bamboo strip to the next. When she got midway, Su Phan looked at the long stretch she still must cross, and her heart thudded even more. But she had to go either forward or back. She certainly couldn't stay here on these terrifying strips of bamboo that might flip her downward into the water at any minute.

Shaking and perspiring, she crawled along and at last reached the other side. Now on solid ground, she closed her eyes and breathed deeply, thankful that she had made it across. Her heart was beating wildly. When she'd calmed down, she looked back at the bridge that was still swaying slightly. *I wish my friends were here to see how brave I am,* she thought. She tried not to think of having to cross it again, on her way back.

She was exhausted from walking and the strain of crossing the bridge. She was getting thirsty, too, but there was still a long way to go. She picked up a large stick to use as a cane, and pretended she was an explorer as she tramped along the path. Large trees and brambles stretched out from both sides, and vines that snaked around trees also rambled across the dirt path, nearly tripping her at times.

She stopped and wiped the perspiration that ran along her cheeks. How many hours had she been walking? She had no idea, and it was hard to tell the location of the sun above the heavy foliage.

If it gets dark I could stray off the path and be lost in the jungle, she thought. *And no one would find me because they wouldn't know where to look.* Swarms of insects began buzzing around her, stinging her face, arms, and legs and adding another measure of misery.

When she finally admitted to herself that she'd been foolish to embark on this venture, the jungle suddenly ended. Right ahead was the clearing the girl had mentioned, and there were the huts. And miracle of miracles, there was her grandmother outside, gathering twigs!

"Ah mah!" Su Phan joyously called out, racing toward the old woman and flinging herself at her. "I'm here!"

The grandmother was so shocked at seeing the girl that she staggered a bit. Then she dropped the twigs and took hold of Su Phan's arms. Her first look of amazement turned into anger.

"I see you are here, Nuisance of My Life," she said. "But why? Has something happened to your family? You're now alone in the world?"

"No, Grandmother. I just wanted to see you."

The woman gave a grunt and stooped to pick up the twigs she had dropped.

Su Phan thought she saw a slight smile at the corners of Grandmother's lips. She took hold of the woman's shirt and followed her into the hut.

"Your ma will be very angry," the old woman said, dropping the twigs in a corner. "I don't suppose you told her of your plans."

"I . . . uh . . . forgot."

The grandmother gave a short laugh. "Well, since you came such a long way I suppose you had better eat and drink. I see you didn't have the sense to bring water."

Su Phan hadn't thought of anything, only her longing to see her ah mah. It didn't matter how much the old woman scolded. Su Phan loved her and needed to be near her.

After she had eaten a bowlful of rice and drunk two cups of water, Su Phan was ready for her talk with Ah mah.

63

"Grandmother," she said, choosing her words carefully, "I do not think you should live in this place."

"Oh?" the woman replied. "And why is that?"

"Because your leaving has made us all very sad."

Her grandmother just sipped her tea.

"In fact, we may become ill with worry." Su Phan slumped a little as though she were already becoming weak. "It is too much for me . . . for us . . . to bear."

Her grandmother eyed her silently for a moment and then gave a short laugh. "If you think that you can coax me with your cute ways as you did your father, you are mistaken. I have moved here and here I will stay."

Genuine tears now welled in Su Phan's eyes. "My father wouldn't want us to be separated. We need you, especially Mother."

Grandmother briefly touched the girl's wrist. "Child, late at night when you were sleeping I talked to your mother. I told her what the villagers have been saying, that it is no longer safe to live there. But she is stubborn, that woman, and would not listen to me."

"So that is why you left us?" Su Phan asked.

"That is why," the old woman said. "Now you must go home before it gets dark. And don't come back here again, or I will tell your ma to tie you up."

Su Phan looked toward the jungle. It was much darker than when she had come. She shivered to think of what lay in wait for her there. Snakes? Even greater swarms of mosquitoes? She was already covered with bites. And the long, swaying bamboo bridge . . . how would she get across it in the dark?

Her grandmother must have read her mind. She

sighed and said, "Come on, little pest. I will see if I can find someone to take you back by boat. Though why I should be concerned about such a nuisance as you I don't know."

She did find a fisherman about to set off. After a whispered conversation, he agreed to take Su Phan home.

She was relieved to see that her mother wasn't back yet from work. But her brother and sister were furious. "We have been looking all over for you, wretched child," Su Lenh said. "How could you go off like that, without telling anyone?"

"If I had told, you wouldn't have let me go," Su Phan replied reasonably.

Su Lenh and Senh Hau shook their heads. What were they to do with such a sister? "I hope at least," her brother said, "that you have learned your lesson."

Su Phan said that she had. She wouldn't go back to see her ah mah. At least not for a couple of weeks. And not without water.

Later that night when they told Mother about Su Phan's trip through the jungle she looked startled but not angry. "My child," she said, "that was a foolish thing to do. I know you miss your ah mah, but believe me, she will come back."

"When?" Su Phan wanted to know.

"When she realizes that there is really no danger here."

Su Phan wanted to believe her mother's words. Something told her, though, that even the grown-ups had no way of knowing what would happen next. Not in a time of war.

Chapter
13

IT WAS NOW 1968 and their teachers had announced at school that the American president, Mr. Johnson, had offered to start peace talks in Paris. Surely the war would soon be over!

But as the days went by, Su Phan didn't know what to believe. The bombing raids were coming closer and they were more deadly. Their neighbors, terrified by reports of deaths from the raids, were moving away.

"Ma," Senh Hau asked one night, "are we going to move, too? Even the school is closing. They have built a new one farther away from here, right in the jungle."

Their mother frowned. "We must stay here because some day your father will come home. If we moved away, he might not be able to find us."

Father had been gone many months now. A great sadness came over Voong Nhi Mui's face whenever she spoke of her husband. "Now," she said, "we will have to trust that we will be safe here."

But a few weeks later, the bombers came even closer to their village. One night Su Phan, her sister, and her brother huddled with their mother in the far corner of the kitchen area behind the empty store as roar after roar split the silence. At last the raid seemed to be over.

"Go upstairs to bed now," Mother said. She picked up the cup of tea she had started to drink before the bombs fell, and then set it down again. "The tea has grown cold," she said. "Like my spirit."

Su Phan went to her mother, stooped beside her by the fire, and put an arm around her. "Life will become warm again," she said.

Absently, her mother patted Su Phan's hand and said, gazing into the fire, "Go to bed, child."

There is no comforting Ma, Su Phan thought. *She will never be happy until our father is returned to us.*

Su Phan sat on the edge of her wooden box bed. She combed her long black hair, which now reached halfway down her back. *Before long, I will not be a child anymore, but a young woman,* she thought. But she would never catch up with her sister, whose hair now came to her waist.

Yawning, Su Phan swung her legs up on the bed. Just as she was reaching upward for the mosquito netting she heard another wave of airplanes approaching. Bombers? And if so, whose?

She hadn't long to wonder. There were whistling sounds, followed almost immediately by blasts so loud

67

they seemed to tear the night apart. Along with the blasts came blinding flashes of light. And then a loud swooshing sound roared right into the house, followed by a dull thud just beneath her. Su Phan lay trembling with fear. When her sister asked, "Are you all right?" Su Phan could only whimper a reply.

As quickly as they had come the bombers were gone. In the sudden silence their mother was heard praying thanks that they had been spared.

Su Phan didn't know how close she had come to being injured until the next day. "Look at that," she said to her sister and brother. "That sound I heard was a piece of shrapnel." She pointed to a chunk of jagged metal lodged in her bed board. "If I hadn't gotten into bed just before, it would have hit me!" She shuddered. "It might have cut off my legs!"

"Close call," her brother agreed.

After the remaining villagers saw the huge craters the bombs had created the night before and heard about the injuries to a man and a boy who had been running home when a bomb fell near them, many more families decided to move away.

Now Su Phan's mother agreed that they, too, must leave. "I will have to find some other kind of work," she said. "And soon I'll go to visit your father and tell him where we have moved." She sighed. "I have no choice. I must protect you children."

They now had so few possessions that it was not difficult to move. They simply wrapped up their bowls and utensils and clothing in bundles and carried them off through the jungle.

Along with some of their neighbors, they headed for an area they thought would be safe . . . as safe as any place in these times. Su Phan was happy to see it was in the same general direction as the place where her ah mah lived. It was also near the sea, and that pleased Su Phan. She knew she'd never like to live where she couldn't see water and feel sea breezes as she went about her daily routine.

The people who already lived in the settlement welcomed the new arrivals and even helped them erect shelters.

Su Phan, who had become used to the coldness of her old neighbors and the taunts of many of her classmates, was pleased by the smiles and warmth that greeted her and the family. "Isn't it wonderful?" she said to Senh Hau. "These people like us."

"Huh. Wait until they find out our father is in prison and why. Then we'll see if they still like us."

"In that case," Su Phan said, "we had better get our house put together quickly, before they do find out."

Her brother shook his head and smiled. "Sometimes you actually make sense," he said to her.

They wasted no time gathering long lengths of sturdy bamboo from the jungle and whatever large pieces of wood they could find from old, deserted houses. The wood became supports for the bamboo sides of their house and braces for the roof. The roof itself was made of huge dried weeds, also gathered from the jungle. Every member of the family helped assemble the necessary building materials. When they had found enough bamboo stalks, they used vines to bind them together.

Then they hoisted the bundles to their shoulders and carried them back to the settlement.

Su Phan got very tired and her legs and shoulders ached by the end of the day, but she said nothing. She knew this work had to be done, and quickly, so they'd have shelter.

Their house was erected in a few days. Then they took mud from the riverbank to cover the rough dirt floor. They smoothed one side of the floor with mud, and when it had dried, they did the other side.

In no way could this home compare with the one they'd left. It was a shelter, and nothing more. There was no comfort in it. But the worst part here in the jungle was the mosquitoes. They were bad enough during the day, but at sunset they swarmed in like dark clouds.

"You'll get used to the mosquitoes," a girl who had lived there for a while told Su Phan. "Before long you won't even notice them."

Su Phan didn't think that would happen. The only thing to do was stay close to the fire, which they kept smoking with damp grass to drive away the flying pests.

It was too far for Su Phan's mother to go to the place where she had worked before. She decided to make *dim sum*—little packets of vegetables and fish wrapped in rice dough—to sell to the people in a larger village nearby. Each day she and Su Phan's sister got up before dawn and cooked. Then they put the dim sum into baskets, got into a borrowed boat, and rowed across an inlet of the sea to the village, which was just around a curve in the shoreline.

Su Phan and Senh Hau also got up at dawn and prepared their school lunch. Then they lit torches made of long sticks, took their books and food containers, and set off.

The walk to the jungle school was long and frightening. Other children had told them of seeing wild boars and snakes along the shadowy path. One boy even claimed to have seen a tiger, but no one believed him.

Su Phan was terrified of snakes. Often her brother, trudging along behind her, yelled, "Watch out! There's a snake! Don't move!"

But Su Phan would scream and run, stumbling and tripping over roots that sprawled over the moist, overgrown path. Then her brother, picking up her food container and handing it to her, would laugh and say, "You are so simpleminded, Su Phan. You believe everything you hear."

After a while she learned to pay no attention to her brother's false warnings. In fact, she'd swing around with her torch and say, "Where's the snake? Pick it up and I'll roast it for your lunch."

One day when her brother shouted a warning, Su Phan just walked on. She caught her bare foot on an especially large root lying on the path. *Then the root moved!*

She looked down and saw that the root was a snake. Frozen in fear, she couldn't budge. But the snake crawled from under her foot and slithered off the path.

"What's the matter with you? I shouted a warning!" her brother yelled, coming up beside her. "Are you all right?"

Su Phan, unfrozen now, grew very angry. "How could I believe you? You've lied so often!" She would have punched him but her arms were full with the torch, the cap long, and her school books.

"You walk ahead now!" she said. "Then you'll be the one who steps on the next snake. Even if I see it I won't call out!"

"Oh, oh, I'm really scared!" her brother said, laughing.

To get even, Su Phan walked closer and closer behind him, her torch aimed at his shoulders. After a while he felt the heat and whirled around.

"Hey, watch it, Su Phan! What do you think I am, a *voha* that you're trying to roast?" Children often caught the grasshopper-like insects called vohas and roasted them on sticks, like marshmallows.

At school, Su Phan discovered she could make herself into a hero when she talked about the snake. "See these feet?" she said, lifting first one and then the other. "These are the very feet that stepped on it."

"Really? Weren't you scared to death?" her classmates asked.

Su Phan shrugged. "By that big . . . huge . . . *very* huge snake? Not at all. My brother even called out a warning, but I stepped on it anyway."

Just then her brother happened to walk up to the group of children. One of the boys told Senh Hau what his sister had said. "Is this true?" the boy asked.

"It's true," Senh Hau replied. "My sister is very brave."

Su Phan smiled gratefully. Maybe her brother wasn't so bad after all.

Chapter
14

BY NOW, ALMOST THREE YEARS had passed since Su Phan's father had been taken away. *When he comes back,* she thought, *he won't call me Mui Mui anymore. I am not the little girl I used to be.*

Life in the jungle area was hard. Their house did not improve with age. They had no new possessions other than a few pots needed for making the dim sum. They couldn't afford to buy new clothing. The government gave out cloth for making just one shirt and one pair of cotton pants per person each year. By the time the family got new cloth, their old clothing was worn and patched.

Su Phan complained about school to her sister. "The paper now is so rough," she said, "it's almost impossible to write on it. And those pen points stuck into wooden handles break easily. As for the ink, it's so watered down now—"

"Oh, stop your grumbling," Su Lenh said. "At least you get to go to school."

"Get to! Don't you realize how lucky you are, being able to stay at home every day?"

"Lucky? Me?" Her sister turned from where she was kneeling on the floor to put a pot on the fire. "I have to get up at dawn!"

"So do I," Su Phan sniffed. "To go to that stupid school where the teachers are so mean."

Su Lenh leaned back on her heels. "I have to help Ma make dim sum every day. And then we have to row across to the other village to sell the food and buy more supplies. And sometimes—"

"I know, I know," Su Phan interrupted. She had heard all these complaints before. "Sometimes you go to the island to get wild vegetables and then you have to row all the way back . . ." Her voice drifted off. "It still sounds like fun."

"Huh!" Her sister got to her feet. "Someday you'll find out how much fun it is."

Su Phan would find out much sooner than her sister expected.

That night, as they all sat on the floor eating their supper of rice, Mother made an announcement.

"I have decided that tomorrow I will go visit your father in prison. I have been told where he is and how to get there."

Her three children stared at her, astonished.

"It is a very long journey. I will be away for several weeks. But I have a great longing to see Chung Bo. Also,

I must tell him where to find us when he's released."

"Oh, Ma!" Su Phan and the others were happy beyond belief.

"Will our ah mah go with you?" Su Phan asked. She visited her grandmother at least once a week now, since the old woman lived not too far away.

"Your grandmother?" Voong Nhi Mui asked with some surprise. "Of course not. The journey would be too hard for her. She is old and weak."

"Then," Senh Hau said, "I will come with you. You must not go on such a long journey alone."

"No, son. I need you to stay here and protect our house and your sisters. You will stay home from school while I'm away."

Before Su Phan could protest about walking to school through the jungle all by herself, her mother said, "You will remain at home, too, Su Phan, to help your sister make dim sum and take it to market."

Su Phan smiled. The idea of a long holiday from school pleased her very much.

Early the next morning, long before dawn, Voong Nhi Mui awakened her children. "I am setting off now. I'll see you when I come back, whenever that may be."

"Bring back our father!" they all said.

"I will, if that is possible," their mother said. But her eyes showed little hope. She took containers of water and rice and set off on her long journey.

When she was out of sight, Su Lenh turned to her sister. "Come, help me with the food. And you," she shouted at her brother, who was headed toward his bed, "don't even think of going back to sleep. We need water from the well. Go fetch it." She paid no attention when he muttered, "Bossy."

The girls worked steadily until their bamboo baskets were filled with an assortment of dim sum. Then they carried them to the boat that was bobbing on the water.

It had been fun playing in the boat before, but now Su Phan found it was hard work rowing so far. She got tired very quickly.

The sun was just rising when they reached the market town on the other side of the inlet. In a short time they sold all the dim sum.

"So much money!" Su Phan exclaimed as her sister knotted the coins in a cloth. "Could we get a stick of sweet bamboo, or perhaps some sesame candy?"

"No! We need to get supplies to make more food, and some rice as well, if you expect to have a full bowl at mealtime."

On the long row back, Su Phan thought of the days that now seemed so long ago. She had been so happy then, playing with her friends, waiting for her father to return home from the sea with a present of candy. She hadn't been happy now for a long time. When the soldiers took away her father they also took away the life the family had always lived.

Su Phan wondered if, when her father returned, happy times would come back with him. Silently, she prayed that the peace they still talked about at school would really happen. How wonderful it would be if it took place while her mother was visiting her father, and they'd return home together. How happy they would be!

"Su Phan! Row!" her sister said. "Are you still dreaming about sweets?"

"Yes," she said, smiling to herself. "I have sweet dreams." She didn't add that they had nothing to do with candy.

Chapter
15

ONE MORNING SU LENH woke up feeling dizzy. "I have such a headache I can't get up," she said. "Su Phan, please bring me a cold cloth for my head."

Su Phan hurried to do so. As she laid the cloth on her sister's forehead, she said, "We're almost out of water. While our brother goes to the well, should I start making the dim sum?"

"No, no," her sister said, eyes closed. "It's too much for one girl to do. We'll just make twice as much tomorrow."

"Su Phan can come with me to the well," Senh Hau said.

"Yes, go, both of you," their sister said. "I need peace and quiet."

Su Phan and her brother started off on the long hike. At first she thought it was fun, scrambling along the smooth path, crossing little streams by leaping from one boulder to the next. The empty bucket swung on a bamboo pole suspended between her shoulder and her brother's.

Coming back was far less fun. In fact, it was tiresome. The pail was heavy with water now, and the pole seemed to grind into her shoulder. And because her balance was not so sure, she slipped on the mossy boulders as they crossed streams, causing the water to splash around in the bucket.

"Take it easy!" her brother shouted as the bucket swung wildly to and fro. "You spill this and we'll have to walk all the way back to the well for more."

When they finally reached their hut, Su Phan was very tired and wanted to lie down and rest her aching muscles. But her sister, still not recovered, ordered her to gather twigs for the fire and start boiling water for rice and tea. Su Phan heard her friends' voices as they came back from school, and now she envied them their easy lives.

The days dragged on, each of them much like the one before. The only difference came about once a week when the girls, after selling their dim sum, rowed to an island where they gathered wild vegetables like watercress, small onions, and creeping sweet potato leaves. These vegetables gave the dim sum more flavor.

It was after their second trip to this island, when they were rowing home, that they suddenly heard the always-frightening sound of bombers. Su Phan looked anxiously up at the sky.

"Can you see them? Are they headed this way?" Su Lenh asked, rowing frantically.

"No. Yes! I can see them and it looks like they'll fly right over us!" Su Phan felt panic rising in her throat. "Where can we hide?" She looked wildly around, but there was only the sea, with land still very far away. Much too far to reach now.

"I'll put the oars in the boat," Su Lenh said. "We'll have to lie down and pull the vegetables up over us. Then perhaps from high up it will look like an empty boat, drifting."

The two girls burrowed down beneath the long stringy vegetables. In a few moments the planes zoomed overhead. Just as their sound was dying away and the girls thought they were safe, a fresh roaring of airplanes shattered the silence. Finally the last planes were gone, and the sky was empty once more.

The sisters sat up and brushed themselves off. But, when they looked around, there was no land to be seen. They must have drifted far from their course.

"*Bay la!*" Su Lenh wailed, echoing the words of their grandmother. "I have no idea where we are. We are lost!"

"Keep calm," Su Phan said, although she herself was frightened. "I think land is over that way."

They began to row, but even after ten minutes or so no shore could be seen.

"I'm afraid we're going in the wrong direction," Su Lenh finally said, pausing to wipe away streams of sweat that were running down her cheeks. "If we continue we might row straight to the enemy."

Su Phan was terrified. "Are they so near?"

"Who knows? Let's go that way. Yes. The sun is beginning to set. I believe our land lies in that direction."

She was right. They rowed, squinting against the sun, and at last spied land on the horizon. Praying that it was their village and not enemy territory, they continued to row. Soon they saw familiar-looking houses.

"Our goddess has protected us," Su Phan said as they finally reached the shore.

They tied up the rowboat, gathered the wilted vegetables in their arms, and stumbled back to their hut.

"Where have you been?" Senh Hau shouted. "I thought you had drowned!" He fixed them with a stern look and said, "Ma would be very angry if she knew how you'd been playing around all day!"

The girls looked at their hands, sore from rowing, and then at their brother.

"Senh Hau, go stick your face in the mud!" Su Lenh suggested.

"Yes, and after that, bring us some tea to our beds," Su Phan added.

Their brother, realizing when he saw the blisters on their hands that his sisters had had a very bad day, brought them tea. "But," he said with a little smile, "I'm not going to stick my face in the mud."

A month passed. Then six weeks. Still, their mother did not return.

"*Bay la!*" exclaimed their grandmother, who had come with her friend to visit. "I traveled here hoping to see my son, but you say you have had no word of him or your mother. Something bad has surely happened. They must have killed Chung Bo!"

"Grandmother, calm yourself," Senh Hau said. His voice trembled, however, and he wouldn't meet the looks of his sisters.

"And your mother has been set upon by thieves and killed also!" The old woman dropped to her hands and knees and swayed back and forth, moaning. Her gray hair slipped from its knot and strands fell about her face, but she seemed not to notice.

"Come, Ah mah," Su Lenh said, kneeling beside her grandmother. "Come into the house and I will make tea for you and your friend. I am sure nothing bad has happened. Mother herself said it is a long journey. Soon she will return, and perhaps Father as well."

At last Grandmother ceased her crying and got shakily to her feet. She had grown to look very old these last few years. Her body was bent over and her eyesight was failing.

After two days Grandmother and her friend decided to go back to their own homes.

"You will let me know of your parents' safe return," Ah mah said, as they set off. "May it be soon, while I am still here to rejoice."

Another couple of days passed and then one evening, staggering with weariness, their mother stumbled into the house. She was alone.

"Oh, my children," she gasped, putting her arms around them and leaning heavily on Su Lenh. "Such a hard, hard journey. I thought at times that I would never have the strength to return to you."

"Poor mother . . ." Su Phan soothed. "Rest, rest."

They helped her to her bed, where she lay down, sighing heavily. "So tired . . . so tired . . ." she moaned.

"Ma, did you see our father?" Senh Hau asked.

"I saw him," she said, eyes closed. "Yes, I saw your father. He is skin and bones. His hair is now gray. He looks old. Very old."

Su Phan asked, "When will he return?"

"Return?" Her eyes opened briefly. "I cannot tell you that. They say he has not yet learned his lesson. He must stay there longer."

The three of them exchanged worried looks. Then Su Lenh said, "Mother, I will prepare food for you. You must be very hungry."

"I am too tired to eat," she said. "Just bring me some hot tea." But she fell asleep before she could take even a sip.

The children gathered around the cooking fire. Sadness lay like a gray cloak on their shoulders. Su Phan had hoped the delay in their mother's return meant their father was about to be released. But she had been wrong.

"He will never return. They will keep him until he dies," Senh Hau said, voicing all their doubts. Su Phan looked at him with blazing eyes. "Don't say such a thing! We'll see our father again. If not this year, then the next!"

Senh Hau twisted his lips but said nothing more.

Su Lenh said dully, "I should prepare something to eat." But she made no move to get up. They all continued to sit, saying little, but looking over at their mother when she groaned in her sleep.

"We should let Grandmother know that Ma has returned," Su Phan said.

"You go do it," her brother said. "Since you like to run to her house whenever you can."

"I will. But not today. I want to be here when Mother wakes up." That was the truth. But it was also true that her own sorrow was enough for now. She hadn't the strength to support and try to comfort her ah mah when she learned that her son would not be coming home soon. Su Phan wouldn't even let herself think the words *if ever.* Surely someday . . . someday. In the meantime they would just have to do the best they could. And wait. Always wait.

As soon as their mother had recovered her strength she insisted that Senh Hau and Su Phan return to school. "Your father wishes you to learn," she said. "Someday this war will be over and then perhaps there will be better things for you to do."

Senh Hau complained to his sister as once again they trudged through the jungle. "What good does it do me to learn reading and spelling and math and history and science?" he grumbled. "Soon I will be a soldier and go off to the war." After a moment he added, "No matter how many times they tell us at school that peace will be here soon, I do not believe it."

Su Phan had looked with pity at boys as young as fourteen who were being rounded up and marched off to join the army. Now she said, "They won't take you, Senh Hau. Even though we must pretend to be Communists in the classroom, the officials must know about our father. So they wouldn't trust you to be loyal and fight."

"No? Then they'd throw me in prison instead."

These words were like a knife in Su Phan's heart. She

didn't want to believe them. Yet, she knew that could happen. In these times, when war was all around them, awful things occurred every day. Bombs fell, villages were burned, people were dragged away, never to return. Would it ever end?

Chapter
16

ONE SEPTEMBER DAY in 1969, school was interrupted by a local Communist official who came into the classroom and spoke quietly to the teacher.

Su Phan was frightened when their teacher broke into sobs.

What had happened? Had their teacher's husband or her family been killed? Had North Vietnam lost the war? The students waited in fearful silence.

The official left and the teacher wiped her eyes before announcing, "Children, I have very sorrowful news. Our leader, Ho Chi Minh, has died."

Su Phan gasped along with the other students. Could this be? Could Uncle Ho have deserted them in these troubled times by dying?

"You will all go home and mourn with your families for two days," the teacher said. "And you will pin a black ribbon to your shirt and wear it for a month, to show respect."

In ordinary times, the children would have been over-joyed at a two-day release from school. But on this day they filed out silently, with heavy hearts.

Even on the walk home there was little talking. Su Phan wondered how this would affect her family.

For two days the entire village was hushed. Families burned incense and spoke prayers. In addition to the sadness over losing their leader, people were concerned. Would their village be taken over by enemy forces? Would they all be killed?

But the two days of mourning passed, and then a month, and nothing seemed to change.

Each year their mother continued to make the long journey on foot to see her husband, Chung Bo, in prison. And each time she returned with the same news: "They say they must keep your father still longer."

After each trip Mother seemed much older and weaker. Her children were worried about her.

"Next time I will go with you," Senh Hau said. But Mother would not hear of it.

"When they see how old you are, and not in the army, they will seize you, too," she said.

"If the army recruiter comes to the school again he could take me as well," Senh Hau replied. "I am fifteen, and boys younger than I have been recruited." He straight-ened his shoulders. "It would be much safer if I stopped going to class. Besides, I have already learned as much as I need to know."

Their mother, clasping her hands together, looked very upset. "But then, what would you do?"

Su Lenh spoke up. "Our brother could go out with the fishermen before dawn, and this would keep him away all day. At night there is not so much danger of the army searching for more soldiers."

Su Phan suspected that her brother and sister had discussed this plan privately. It sounded like a good one, and their mother finally agreed.

The plan worked well. The villagers, who could have reported the young man in their midst, didn't do so. It might have been because of pity for his mother. But more than likely it was because Senh Hau was a good fisherman and each night brought back desperately needed food for the villagers.

Now Su Phan went to school alone. At the age of almost thirteen, because her schoolwork had improved, or perhaps because she had lost some of her spirit, she was finally awarded the red tie. Ho Chi Minh was gone, but his memory was still honored.

Two more years dragged by without change. Su Phan entered her final year of school, but was unable to complete it.

One day she came home to find her mother lying in bed. "What is it?" she asked her sister. "What's wrong with Ma?"

"The work and worry have exhausted her," Su Lenh said. "But most of all, she's sick at heart. I'm afraid she's given up hope that our father will ever return." Su Lenh sighed. "After all, it's been nearly seven years. Ma no longer has the strength to go see him, nor even the strength to carry on each day. I don't know what to do."

Seven years? Had it really been that long? Su Phan had lost track of time, with one dull day succeeding another. But by now her own hair had grown down to her waist and she had become a young woman. Her sister was of marriageable age, but who could think of weddings in these times?

"I know one thing," Su Phan said. "I'm going to stay home from now on. Together we'll do Ma's work, just as we did each time when she went away."

Their mother was too weak to object. She rested while her daughters made dim sum and rowed across the bay to sell them at the market each day. When they returned they helped her with the cooking and cleaning. Mostly, their mother worked outside in the small garden. The vegetables helped make the rice and fish go further for their meals, but growing them required much water.

It was now Su Phan's job to go to the well several times a week. Being bigger and stronger, she carried two buckets of water suspended on a pole over her shoulder. It still seemed a long way to go, and her shoulder ached from the weight. When the hurt became too strong, she'd carefully lower the buckets, rest, then shift the pole to her other shoulder.

There was one chore, though, that she looked forward to with pleasure. Once a week she and Su Lenh took their laundry, as well as some of their neighbors' laundry, in a basket to a stream and waterfall a mile or so away. It was a beautiful, hidden spot, so far untouched by war.

They liked to sit on the rocks by the stream, dangle their legs in the rippling water, and listen to birds singing in the greenery all about them.

After they'd washed the clothes the sisters would rest again and talk about what they'd do when the war ended.

"I'm going to marry and have lots of children," Su Lenh said, with a dreamy look in her eyes.

"Not me. I want to travel to China where our ancestors lived and died," Su Phan said, "I'll visit relatives still living there. And who knows? After that I might travel even farther, to see some of the lands I've read about in school."

"You wouldn't leave us!" her sister said in alarm.

"Just for a while. Then I'll come back here to be with my family."

"If we're still alive," Su Lenh said glumly. "Who knows? We may all be dead tomorrow."

"And wet today!" Su Phan said as she playfully pushed her sister into the water. Laughing, she jumped in after her. Then they waded over and around the big rocks to stand under the waterfall. It was icy cold and they couldn't stay under very long. They shook the water off their long black hair and waded back to the basket of clothing. After wringing out their shirts and pants, they picked up the laundry and started home. All too soon the heat and humidity took away the good, cool feeling.

"I wonder what snow is like," Su Phan said one day, rubbing her cheek against her shoulder to wipe off the sweat. "In a book we read one day at school, it said snow is very cold and white as it falls from the sky. I can't picture it."

"It is only a story," Su Lenh said. "Someone's imagination. There is no such thing." She jerked on her handle of the basket. "Pay attention, Su Phan. You're making me carry most of the weight."

"My arm is so tired," Su Phan complained. "Let's set the basket down for just a moment. Then we can trade sides so our other arms can carry the load." She rubbed her shoulder. "The basket wouldn't be so heavy if it were only our few clothes inside."

"I know," Su Lenh agreed. "But we need the rice our neighbors give us in exchange for doing their laundry."

As they sat, Su Phan pulled up a strip of sweet grass and chewed on the end. "Someday things will be different. I shall be different, too, when I go to other lands."

Her sister heaved a sigh. "There you go with your daydreaming again! Can't you be content with life as it is, or will be once this war is over?"

"No. There is too much in the world to see. How can I be content to live all my life in one place?"

"So you really would go away and leave your family, your country?"

"Perhaps not forever. But no matter what, my family will always remain in my heart."

"Your heart!" Su Lenh said angrily. "What about Father?"

"I would wish to see our father, of course. If he returns."

"If!" Su Lenh leaped to her feet. "You say *if* he returns. Sister, I think you *have* no heart!"

Su Phan stood up and furiously took hold of the basket. Of course she had a heart, and she loved her father as much as ever. Often she had imagined what it would be like, the day he returned. There he would come, over the hills surrounding the village, and then he'd break into a run as he spied his family outside their house. And he'd laugh his strong laugh, and sweep them into his arms!

But she was beginning to wonder if this would ever happen. Would her father survive the hardships of prison life and come back to them?

Chapter
17

ONE DAY IT TOOK THE GIRLS longer than usual to finish the laundry. It was heavier this week, with more neighbors adding their clothing to the load.

On the way back, they rested halfway home, sitting on a tiny hillock beside the path. Even though the sun beat down relentlessly, the earth under the weedy grass was still damp from the morning's rain.

Su Phan closed her eyes briefly. When she opened them she saw her sister shielding her eyes with her hand and looking ahead where the path forked.

"What is it?" Su Phan asked. "What are you looking at?"

"That old man coming down the other path. I don't remember seeing him in the village."

Su Phan squinted into the distance and shrugged. "He's probably someone's grandfather, coming to pay a visit." She stood up. "Let's go."

They picked up the basket of wet laundry, which now seemed heavier than before, and struggled toward the fork in the path. As they reached it, the old man, leaning heavily on a stout stick, reached it, too. He stopped and wiped his perspiring face with a rag.

"Good afternoon," Su Lenh said in the polite voice reserved for elders.

"Good afternoon to you," the old man said, his voice creaking. He swayed slightly and looked confused.

"Are you lost?" Su Phan asked. "Or are you headed for the village this path leads to?"

"I am looking . . ." He coughed, then said, "Do you girls by chance know Voong Nhi Mui?"

The sisters edged closer together. Who was this stranger who was asking about their mother? What did he want?

"Why . . ." Su Phan hesitated. ". . . do you ask for her?"

The old man wiped his forehead. "Because I am Chung Bo, her husband."

The girls stared, unable to speak. Then Su Phan stammered, "You are Chung Bo?" As she said the words, something in the man's eyes stirred her memory. Her heart began to beat very rapidly. Then with great joy, she shouted, "We are your daughters!"

"My daughters!" he gasped. Then, with tears pouring down his cheeks, he said, "My daughters! I did not recognize my own daughters!" And clutching the girls to him, he said, "But you were so little when I left. I have missed the many years of your growing."

It was their father, but not the same father. Instead of

94

the tall, proud man Su Phan remembered, this one was hunched over and thin, very thin. And his thick black hair was now wispy and gray.

Su Lenh looked confused and distressed as her eyes traveled over the faded shirt and the dirt-smeared black pants of this man who had been away from them for more than seven years. His feet were bare, crusted with mud and clotted blood from brambles and insect bites. Sweat soaked his clothes and streamed down his face, and he gave off the dank smell of the jungle.

But now, tears streamed down all of their faces, tears of sorrow for what had been taken from them, and tears of joy at their reunion. They clasped each other as the tears continued to fall.

At last, their father pulled away from them and said, "Run now to your mother's house and tell her I have returned. I will follow slowly, as I must."

"You go!" Su Phan said to her sister. "Leave the clothes. We can come back for them later. I'll guide Father to our home."

As her sister raced down the path, Su Phan told her father to lean on her. Even so, they had to stop often to rest.

Before long they saw two figures rushing toward them. Their mother, after the first shock at hearing the news, had torn out of the house, with Su Lenh beside her.

When she reached Chung Bo she stopped and stared, still unbelieving. Then she flung herself at him and cried with great happiness. They all embraced, letting go of the sorrow they had kept within their hearts for so many years.

After the girls had retrieved the laundry, they all started toward home. The parents, arms entwined, moved very slowly. Seeing them back together at last, Su Phan felt as though she was floating with happiness.

Chapter
18

WHEN THEY ARRIVED at their house near the edge of the small village, Chung Bo looked at it with some bewilderment. At first Su Phan thought he was only confused, but then she saw it through her father's eyes. Instead of the two-story home he had left in the other village, this house was little more than a thrown-together shelter. It had become even more dilapidated through the years.

As they entered the house a look of dismay crossed her father's face. "This is your home?" he cried. "It is not much better than a place for animals!" Tears once again clouded his eyes. "What have I done to my family?" He collapsed to the dirt floor, hands over his face.

Voong Nhi Mui motioned to her eldest daughter to stir up the fire. "Hush, my husband," she murmured. "We will make you some tea."

"The beautiful things we once had!" Chung Bo

moaned. "The beds, the cupboards. Now there is only . . ." He looked around at the clumsy mats on boards where they slept. There were no furnishings, only cooking utensils stacked in a heap. "What has happened to the things we once had?"

"Sssh," Voong Nhi Mui crooned. "Those things are long gone, and are of no importance. You are back with us. That is all that matters."

Chung Bo accepted the cup of tea his daughter handed him and took a sip. Then he set down the cup. "Where is my son? Is he at school?"

"Senh Hau will be here soon," Voong Nhi Mui said, giving her daughters a look that meant they should be silent.

"And you, Su Lenh, why are you not at school?" the father asked, bewildered. "My children must be educated. It is what I have always wished."

"I am too old for school now," the older girl said.

Before her father could question her, Su Phan said, "Grandmother doesn't know that father has returned! Shall I run and tell her?"

"It is getting too dark to go that distance now," her mother said. "Our good news can wait till morning. Besides, your father is very tired. He should rest before he faces more excitement."

There was more excitement, however, when Senh Hau came home and stood in the doorway, bringing with him the smell of fish. He stared at the scene, confused.

"Who is this man?" Chung Bo whispered to Su Phan. "Do I know him?"

"Father, this is Senh Hau, your son."

"My son!" The old man got to his feet and hobbled forward.

As he approached Senh Hau, the boy shrank back. "Who are you?" he asked as the man reached out to embrace him. "Oh no!" He stared at his mother and then back at the man. "Oh . . . can it be true? Is this . . . is this my father?" And then, they flung themselves into each other's arms.

Pulling apart, the two men gazed at each other. Seeing his father so bent and his face so dry and wrinkled, Senh Hau said, "Oh, Father, what have they done to you?"

The old man shook his head. "Most of all, they have stolen your childhood from me," he said. "I was not here for your growing up. I did not know my own daughters when I saw them."

Then he looked at Su Phan with blurred eyes. "Mui, Mui," he said. "Little girl, do you remember how you used to sing for your father?"

"Yes, Pa. I remember. But I have not sung now for many years."

"Ah," he said sadly, "so they have taken that away as well."

The welcome Chung Bo received from his family didn't extend to the people in the village.

"Why do they turn away when I approach them?" Chung Bo asked his family. "Do they think I carry some dread disease?"

"Father," Senh Hau said, "it's because they're afraid."

"Afraid of an old man?"

"No," Senh Hau said, "it is only politics. While you have been away, the Communists have taken over everything." His voice dropped to a whisper. "Outwardly, our family has seemed loyal to this regime. If people have not really believed us, at least they have pretended to do so. And why not? We have served the village well. We have supplied our neighbors with vegetables from our garden and with fish that I have caught. We don't cause trouble."

"But now that I have returned?"

Senh Hau shifted uneasily. "They know where you have been all these years and have guessed why you were in prison. It makes them uneasy." He patted his father's hand. "Don't be distressed. They'll soon forget about all that. Life is hard. People are too concerned about making a living to think very long about their neighbors."

Chung Bo only nodded.

Su Phan, listening, felt sad for her father. She didn't tell him that she and her sister did laundry for the people of the village in exchange for rice. She didn't want to further injure the pride of this man who had once been a prosperous trader. It was hard, she knew, for him to accept the fact that his family was now almost destitute.

In the days that followed, her father slowly regained some of his strength, although he could never again be the man he once was. He had quiet talks with his wife and with his mother, who said that now that she had seen her son once again, she could die in peace and go to live with her ancestors.

Some weeks later, after the evening meal, Chung Bo lit his pipe and called his family to join him. "I have thought it all out," he said. "We don't need to stay in this place. Your grandmother has told us there are empty huts in the area where she lives. Let us move there, and start afresh, where people don't know our history."

In other times, Su Phan would have been sorry to leave her friends, but she had none here. Her old companions, Khenh and Lien, had married and moved away. She hadn't seen Peng in years. She was glad her family was going to move to a place where she could see her grandmother every day.

The old woman was overjoyed at the news that her family would be near her. "My neighbors here will make you welcome," she said.

"Or," Su Phan said with a laugh, "they will feel your switch."

Grandmother only grunted, but a smile hovered on her lips.

Life was more pleasant in their new surroundings. Su Phan's parents relaxed a little and began to feel more hopeful. They planted and tended a large vegetable garden and raised pigs and chickens. The girls continued to make and sell dim sum and their brother continued to fish. One day was much like another, and the family settled into a routine. *I want life to go on this way always,* Su Phan thought. *I don't want anything to change.*

But in her heart she knew this couldn't be. Life always changed, no matter what you wanted.

Chapter
19

ONE NIGHT AFTER THEIR MEAL, the family sat around the fire, as usual. Grandmother, who often shared dinner and stayed the night now, began talking of the old days in China.

"Much has happened in my lifetime," she said, "some good, some bad. But now I am content. I am with my family on earth. And soon I will go to join my ancestors."

Su Phan, who was seated next to her grandmother, put her arm around the old lady's frail shoulders. "Don't speak of leaving us," she said. "We could not live without our ah mah."

Surprisingly, the woman who seldom showed affection took Su Phan's hand and kissed it. "You are a good girl," she said, "if sometimes a foolish one. Do not ask me to stay, however, when it is time for me to take my leave."

Just two nights later the old woman died quietly, in her sleep.

The family wept and put on white clothing to show their grief, as was the Chinese custom. They burned much incense, and sobbed as they laid their dear ah mah to rest.

Su Phan visited her grave each day and brought fresh flowers from their little garden.

"Grandmother," she said, kneeling on the bare earth, "when this war finally ends, I will cover your grave with flowers. We will rejoice in spirit, you and I."

When the war did end, in 1975, it caught everyone off guard.

Su Phan, sweeping the floor of their house, heard shouting outside and the firing of guns. She began to tremble. Was the South Vietnamese army advancing, looting and burning? She must get her parents, who were working in the garden, and flee with them into the jungle!

But when she dashed from the house, she saw her ma and pa clinging to each other, crying. At the same time, however, they were laughing. *Why?* she wondered.

"Mui, Mui," her father shouted, forgetting she was no longer a child, "rejoice with us! The war is over!"

Su Phan looked from them to the villagers, dancing and shouting. Was this real, or was it just another rumor of peace?

Her sister, Su Lenh, came running down the path, water sloshing from the pails suspended from a pole over her shoulder. She, too, was joyous. "Good news! The war has ended," she called as she came close. "I heard it on my way back from the well. Have you heard, too?"

"We have, but it's more than I can believe," Su Phan said.

Several neighbors rushed toward them and grabbed their hands and whirled them around.

"How do people know this is true?" Su Phan asked when she had caught her breath.

"Soldiers passing through on their way back home have told us. The fighting is over."

A little while later their brother surprised them by dashing into the village. "Some fishermen shouted the news to us!" he said. "There will be no more work done today. Everyone is celebrating!"

At last Su Phan could believe it was finally over. She joined in the merriment that went on far into the night and continued the next day. All cares were forgotten, all fears had vanished. The war was indeed was over, and they had survived!

For a while, lying in bed at night, Su Phan still trembled at the sound of airplanes flying over. But in time, as good news continued to flow into the village, she knew the airplanes were just returning to their bases. The war that none of them had really understood, and that had swallowed up so much of their lives, was indeed over.

Carrying out her promise, Su Phan went to her grandmother's grave and covered it with flowers.

Peace did not bring an end to change, however. Only months later, marriage and ambition took Su Phan's sister and brother away to distant towns.

At the age of seventeen, Su Phan also married and went to live in her husband's village nearby.

Not long after, with sorrow, she took leave of her parents and went with her husband to Hong Kong, a place she knew nothing about. Eventually, circumstances took them to far-off America, a country she had once feared, but which now seemed full of hope and promise.

Soon, her life was filled with the demands and challenges of living in a large city. Su Phan had her own children now, and her days were so filled with household cares that she had no time to think of times long past.

But at night when she was asleep, she dreamed of her faraway childhood. She was traveling through the jungle on her way to school, hearing her brother's teasing laugh. She was with Su Lenh at the waterfall, breathing in the greenery and bird songs. Once again, she was with her mother, talking softly as they made tea by the evening fire.

But most often in her dreams she was standing on the shore watching her father's ships come floating back through the mists overhanging the sea. Soon she would wave and he would wave in return. Then he would step ashore and carry her to their home. Later, he would light his pipe and say, "Mui, Mui, come sing for your father."

And she would sing.

Afterword

Su Phan (who has changed her name to Fay) now lives in Chicago with her three teenage children. Her mother died in Vietnam, and her father came to live with Fay and her family until his death in November 1995.

Su Lenh now lives in China. Senh Hau and his family are in Ho Chi Minh City (Saigon). Fay keeps in touch with her sister and brother by mail and by phone.

Fay occasionally hears from her childhood friends. Two of the women still live in Vietnam and one has emigrated to Canada.

At present, besides working in a beauty salon, Fay studies English and takes computer courses.

She met her co-author at the Literacy Center in Chicago. In the course of improving her English, Fay told her story, bit by bit, and wrote it down. She hopes that through this book her very Americanized children will understand what it was like when their mother was young and lived in Vietnam, a country torn by war.